ANOTHER LOOK AT ST. JOHN'S GOSPEL

Ivan Clutterbuck

Foreword by
the Abbot of Elmore

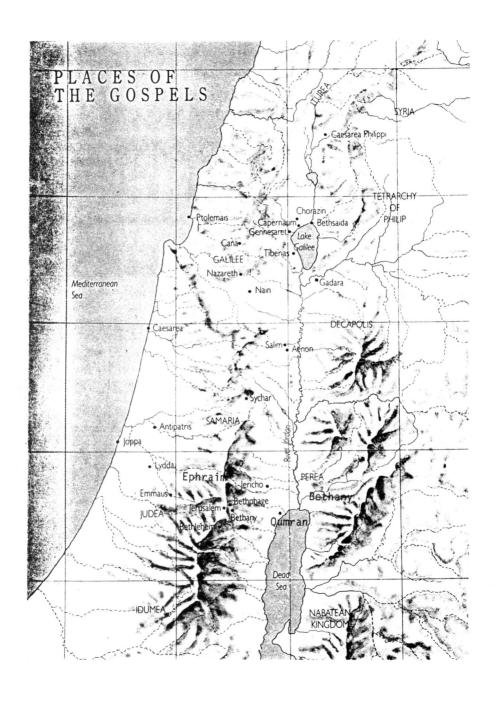

PLACES OF
THE GOSPELS

ITUREA

SYRIA

Caesarea Philippi

TETRARCHY
OF
PHILIP

Chorazin
Ptolemais
Capernaum   Bethsaida
Gennesaret Lake
Cana   Galilee
GALILEE   Tiberias
Nazareth

Mediterranean
Sea

Nain
Gadara

Caesarea

DECAPOLIS

Salim   Aenon

Sychar

Antipatris
SAMARIA

Joppa

Lydda
Ephraim   Jericho   PEREA
Emmaus   Bethphage   Bethany
JUDEA   Jerusalem
Bethlehem   Bethany   Qumran

River Jordan

Dead
Sea

IDUMEA

NABATEAN
KINGDOM

CONTENTS

FOREWORD

St. John's Gospel tells us of the beginning and the end. Its theme is sublimely summarised in the Prologue, which might also be called an epilogue. The startling transition in verse 19 of the first chapter alerts the listener to what is perhaps the most primitive witness to Jesus and to his early ministry, to a tradition upon which the so-called synoptic gospels may ultimately be based. For St. John's Gospel seems to span a lifetime. Relegated by some to a position of a 'late' gospel – anything from 96 AD onwards – its dating is now in process of being reassessed. John Robinson, however, refused to date it, and spoke of a "procedural priority" (*The Priority of John*, p. 5*). This tantalising phrase should excite all who wish to study the New Testament with a view to sharing the faith of its writers.

As St. Benedict's Rule aspires to be no more than a "little rule for beginners", so Ivan Clutterbuck wants his book to introduce its readers to the wonders of the Evangelist's narrative. He takes seriously the early Palestinian tradition, as well as the important development of that tradition in the unfolding life of the Church.

I recommend this little guide on St. John's Gospel and hope that it will lead its students to those 'loftiest of heights of doctrine and devotion'.

Dom Basil Matthews, OSB,
Abbot of Elmore.

*"... may well have begun earlier *and* gone on later than the synoptics".

INTRODUCTION

This is a small book for a large subject. However, I hope to tempt those who do not have very much time for reading to take another look at St. John's Gospel. This has always been a much – loved book for Christians but its historical value has been overlooked. A recent book, The Bible Without Illusions by the Hanson brothers (SCM), is forthright when it says, "As we read the Fourth Gospel we must be aware of the fact that the author is capable of distorting or moulding historical facts for his own purposes and is recording the post-resurrection impression of Christ as if it were the pre-resurrection history".[1] Thus it has been discounted as sound history and not generally used in the classroom for examination purposes. Rather have the Synoptic Gospels been preferred.

However, in recent years this verdict on St. John has been changing and it is now being said that we must take very seriously the historical, social and geographical details peculiar to narratives found only in the Fourth Gospel. In a notable book, Christian Origins (SPCK 1985) Christopher Rowland sums up the present situation. He writes, "Few would deny that in its present form and style the Gospel of John stands apart from the others. It has been dubbed the 'spiritual Gospel', and many have been convinced that we have in this text a sophisticated theological exposition of the significance of Jesus of Nazareth in which the reporting of the incidents of Jesus' life takes second place to theological exposition. For a long time, it was considered that the lack of concern for historical reporting in the Gospel meant that the Evangelist had simply taken over incidents and sayings from one or more of the other Gospels and used them in his presentation of the impact of Jesus. While no one will doubt the sophistication of Johannine theology, it represents a strange reversal of fortunes that the 'spiritual Gospel' has been rehabilitated as a document of some worth for the historian whereas its companion Gospels have suffered the fate of having doubts cast upon their historical reliability".[2]

I have quoted Rowland at some length because I believe it has exciting possibilities both for teaching and evangelism. For example if I were back in the classroom now I would want to present Our Lord's life to the senior school through the eyes of St. John rather than of the Synoptics. I would do this not only for theological reasons but because the Fourth Gospel is one of movement from one end of Palestine to another. We find Jesus over three years making friends and enemies in both Jerusalem and Galilee. A change of scene is always helpful when holding the interest of the classroom.

New respectability for John must be exciting for evangelism because this gospel is one of revelation and witness and no programme of mission can be successfully presented without those two ingredients at the centre. In an essay, The Priest As Teacher (Additional Curates' Society), published a short time ago I said that any programme of re-evangelisation must depend on a correct balance between proclamation (kerugma) and teaching (didache). In other words the shattering facts of the Lord's saving work for us must be proclaimed first and then we must teach people how to change their lives accordingly. This was the method of the first apostles. In recent years, however, we seem to have been clever at different techniques of teaching but have been short of proclamation. I hope another look at St. John's Gospel may awaken Christians to the fact that they have a well-documented message to proclaim.

I have tried, therefore, to produce a guide to other men's scholarship and this I hope will be useful in schools and parishes as well as for the ordinary layman. It could also provide material for lay apostolate study. In this I have been helped very much by John Robinson's posthumous work, The Priority of John (SCM 1985). He had no doubt that John's Gospel was early and written by an eye-witness and, as a vice-principal of a theological college said to me, nobody has answered him yet. But I have also consulted commentaries by other scholars and have learnt much. It is clear that my small work cannot be a commentary but I have singled out passages which I felt had profited from an early date.

Finally I hope St. John's Gospel will be studied verse by verse and that my notes will encourage others to add their insights.

Ivan Clutterbuck

STRAIGHT FROM THE HORSE'S MOUTH

Suitably on April 1st recently, the BBC put out a TV documentary which claimed to show that Hitler had been in England in 1936. It showed a faded photo of him looking out of a window with Unity Mitford, a devoted follower. Convincing detective work was employed to show that this incident took place in the East End of London. Lamp posts in the foreground had a special design and had been tracked down to the Stepney area where, in that year, Oswald Mosley had held a march of Black Shirts. Attention was drawn to the casement windows from which Hitler was looking and it was stated that these could not be German because the style was not found there. So, Hitler had quietly come to England and according to an even more faded photo had met the king. This report was developed further to produce the theory that he had lent the Prime Minister a large sum of money to help with our unemployment. So later Neville Chamberlain had been forced to respond by signing the Munich agreement in 1938.

It all sounded good stuff and witnesses from Hitler's domestic staff added credibility. Undoubtedly history would have to be re-written if this revelation was true. However, I was a bit doubtful about those windows because, as a schoolboy, I had stayed in the Black Forest in a hotel which had casement windows. Then suddenly the whole affair exploded in our faces because the TV narrator said the convincing German witnesses, a butler and a maid, had been arrested for fraud in another matter and were not to be trusted in the Hitler affair. It was all revealed as a hoax and history did not have to be changed.

I have started these notes on St. John's Gospel with that story because I believe it has something to teach us about the way some of our Biblical criticism has been conducted over a very long period of time. Attitudes have sometimes been taken on unproven evidence and false premises. It all started about two hundred years ago as part of the Age of Enlightenment when scholars, first on the Continent, later in this country, became more excited with the intellectual skill of man rather than with the revelation of God found in the Bible and the Church. After success in plumbing the mysteries of science, they turned to examine the Scriptures and here they found much which contradicted their recent discoveries in other fields. The account of Creation, miracles and the supernatural came under the magnifying glass and then the life of Our Lord was examined. At first, it was a foreign operation with Germans like Reimarus, Strauss, Baur and others showing that the ministry of Jesus was more a human matter than a divine epiphany. This then sent scholars elsewhere into all directions asking more and more questions and gaining an academic career for life as a result. In time this excitement reached England and we have had a flow of scholars who have not hesitated to be as radical as their German predecessors.

I stepped into this scene when I read Theology in my third year at Cambridge just before the last war. The man of the moment seemed to be B.H. Streeter who had gained fresh significance by his recent death. After demolishing the resurrection in 1912 he had probed deeply into the Synoptic problem and concluded that there were all sorts of sources for someone who wanted to write a Gospel a generation after the original events. He extracted from the Gospel texts a collection of sayings which he named Q which has been much loved by scholars ever since and only recently challenged by Michael Goulder in a book, Alternative Approaches to New Testament Study.[3] In fact it was easy for a student to get the idea that in the early Church there were a number of writers who spent their time copying each other's works and passing them off as original eye-witness account of Jesus' life. To add to the confusion of a simple theological student a new theory called form criticism was being treated with reverence. This sought to discover the Sitz in Leben, or situation in life which had prompted a later generation of Christians to record a saying or miracle of Jesus. From here it might be possible to reach back and discover what Jesus really said and did but it was also an easy step for the critic to suspect that an actual Gospel unit had been created by the later Christian community itself to express their own religious experience. The emphasis on the role of the community has led to radical scepticism on the part of some scholars who hold that very little, if any, of the Gospel sayings can be accepted as genuine. In fact there have been some Oxford scholars since the 1960s who have taught that only six or seven sayings of Jesus can be regarded as authentic.

All this can be disruptive of Christian faith and morals in our present age because if a second generation of Christians can record the Lord's life as they experienced it and not necessarily as it actually happened, then later generations may do the same. So the distinctive revelation of God through Jesus Christ may be lost and we are left dependent chiefly on the spiritual experience of the day for evaluating right and wrong. This has been called situation ethics. I do not think that Church leaders have realised the extent by which the impact of Christian preaching has been undermined by radical Biblical scholars whose theories in some way have influenced most of our Anglican clergy today.

How can a church have a programme of evangelism when the central message of that kind of preaching and teaching has been compromised? It is clear that those who had been with Jesus during his ministry understood they had been entrusted with a revelation never before given to man and one which was final. God in human form had come among them and sent them to preach this good news to all the world. This proclamation or kerugma was desperately preserved against deviant speculation into the second century AD and beyond. In a new book, The Johannine Question, (SCM) Martin Hengel shows how a school of John the Elder about 100 AD fought to preserve the true Gospel against those with different ideas.[4] With such efforts the Church was able to go forward with great confidence until modern times when the integrity of the New Testament seems to be questioned. As a result of this questioning the preaching and teaching of the clergy has suffered. A recent book, The Bible Without Illusions, by RPC and AT Hanson suggests that a common attitude among clergy today is : "Let us accept a moderate dose of biblical criticism. We are not fundamentalists. But we will drop it when it begins to hurt us." The writers then proceed to take apart most of the Bible books, only to say at the end how wonderful they are!

A modern scholar, A.E. Harvey, in a book, Jesus and The Constraints Of History, sums up admirably the prevailing climate of those who today are engaged in a serious and critical study of the New Testament. "The gospels, it is now recognised, can no longer be regarded simply as records ... of what in fact took place. They are rather the product of a situation in which the first, or even second or third generation of Christians found themselves, a situation which not only determined what they chose to preserve out of their traditions and memories of Jesus but also influenced their manner of recording them, forcing them to tell the stories in such a way that their own problems and questions should be met and answered by them and even to introduce material which they doubtless believed to be authentic but which was in reality the product of their own pious reflection upon the remembered origins of their faith". Later he adds, "it carries with it a disconcerting consequence. If the reports about Jesus in the gospels are the creation of the Church, rather than the testimony of eye-witness to the original events, then it is possible to regard any New Testament statement about Jesus as historically unreliable".[5] Harvey then goes on in the rest of his book to show that such pessimism is entirely unfounded.

He is, in fact, only one of recent scholars to turn the tide in favour of the complete reliability of the Gospels. He is joined, for example, by that great scholar C.F.D. Moule who wrote in 1977 that he had written his book, The Origin of Christology, because he had come to be convinced that there were false assumptions behind a good deal of contemporary New Testament scholarship. In particular he casts doubts on the "history of religions" school which described and understood Jesus as a sort of evolutionary process. He says, "In a word, I am concerned to challenge, in the name of the evidence, such a statement as that the fundamental problem of Christology of the New Testament ... was that the view of Jesus found in New Testament Christology was not historically true of Jesus himself".[6] Even more definitely in recent years John Robinson, described as "perhaps all in all the most intellectually skilful ecclesiastic of his generation, a man of very polished scholarship as well of considerable faith", showed that the New Testament was to be trusted. His Redating the New Testament and the Priority of John took the attack into the very midst of those who had written off the reliability of the Gospels. To quote but one of his dismissals of modern pessimistic scholarship, he wrote of redaction criticism, "The history of Jesus is thus reduced to the history of the church's understanding of him. But such a reaction is quite unwarranted".[7]

So at last in our day the teacher is able to present a balanced view of the New Testament and the Gospels in particular. He can come before his class with the text of the greatest set of religious documents in the world and unfold them in such a way that his pupils may draw the utmost value from the kerugma or proclamation of Jesus. They may learn the different ways of handling such books but at any rate they will at least see the text which is more than most of the people of this country have done. It is hoped that they will conclude that they are studying teaching straight from the horse's mouth, if that is not irreverent!

Looking Again at St. John's Gospel

All this preamble is necessary because the Fourth Gospel has suffered more than the others at the hands of Biblical critics. By the time I had ended my theological studies before the last war I had accepted that it had been written in John's extreme old age, ninety at least, and that this work was more a meditation than a serious historical account. Even this was a conservative estimate because some scholars were saying that he had not written it at all but another John of the next generation. The result of this was to make John's Gospel unsatisfactory evidence for the life of Jesus and it has been possible to give portraits of him without quoting this Gospel at all. In his great commentary R.E. Brown notes, "It has been common place in the critical investigation of the historical Jesus that no reliance can be placed on material found in John". He questions this on the ground that it is now clear that John draws on independent and primitive tradition. Lest he should be thought too conservative, however, he goes on to say that we must proceed with care because he believe that the Gospel developed from that original witness in five stages. He leaves no doubt that, in his mind at least, each stage represented a step further away from the primitive tradition".[8] He says further that this limits the ability of the final form of the Gospel to give a scientifically accurate portrait of the Jesus of history.

Brown gives the earliest possible date for the writing of the Gospel as 75 AD and the latest date as 100 – 110AD. In fact any later dates have been ruled out through the discovery of a fragment of papyrus of this Gospel, written about 140 AD. This would mean that the complete book must have been in circulation a considerable time before that.

John certainly differs from the other three Gospels in many aspects and this has led critics to say that either he was correcting them or adding his material to theirs. In other words he relies on the Synoptics. But as Brown implies above it is now thought that he had his own independent sources and owes little to the others. It is now a matter of discovering how he obtained his information and who put them down in writing. Was the author the same man who witnessed the Lord's ministry from close at hand?

The general view even among those who think John wrote independently is that the material was developed over a period of time by later editors. However, in his new book Martin Hengel has come up with the idea that the writer of this Gospel was present in the Jerusalem of Jesus' day and was a close witness of all that the Master said and did.[9] But he was not the simple fisherman, John, who could not have written such an erudite book. Rather is he another John, the beloved disciple, who had connections with the high priestly caste and thus had aristocratic background. This man, Hengel claims, became the charismatic head of a school in Asia Minor and after a long time wrote down or caused to be written our present Fourth Gospel.

Hengel's theory depends very much on the Christian situation round Ephesus at the end of the first century. His book is argued with Germanic thoroughness and uses as evidence the three letters of John which he thinks were written by the same hand as the gospel. The helpful point here is that the gospel is written by an eye witness and not by another hand. I wonder what John Robinson would have said about this theory because in his posthumous book, The Priority of John, he identifies the writer as John the son of Zebedee, the fisherman. As we shall see later he thinks it was written for a circle of Greek Jews round Jerusalem at an early date. In fact the Johannine problem has puzzled scholars more than any others and many are the theories which have been put forward. There are tantalising clues in the narrative about the beloved disciple who could have written the book. Was he John, Mark, Lazarus, John the son of Zebedee or an anonymous disciple?

If I said the scholarship on John's Gospel was so considerable that it was impossible to cover it all I would be in good company for Brevard Charles in the chapter on John in his book, The New Testament as Canon, says "The literature of modern scholarship on the Gospel of John is quite overwhelming and far exceeds any one person's ability to master it".[10]

So what conclusions can I as an ordinary spectator on the side line make? It is important that I should have some opinion because over the years I have had to teach at several levels the Christian faith. In state and private schools, in naval training establishments, in parishes and in further education I have had to give some account of the teaching of Jesus. Am I to exclude the definite evidence which I find in the Fourth Gospel? If so, I am handicapped because John is very forthright in his witness to Jesus as the son of God. For what it is worth, then, I have tried to put some thoughts together hoping they may help other teachers and encourage them to use this Gospel in their teaching programmes.

First may I say I have always been uneasy about a late date for John. How could such a book be written about 90 AD and not be influenced in some way by the catastrophic fall of Jerusalem in 70 AD. Even if this work was written in far away Asia Minor nevertheless such a disaster would have affected Jews everywhere because it was the end of an era. My suspicions about the late date have been voiced by greater theologians and scholars than myself – and here I should say I have no pretentions to professionalism in the subject. I spent most of my time at Cambridge reading Classics. But I was one of C.H. Dodd's first pupils before the war and I can remember his doubts about a late date for John. Temple's famous Readings in St. John's Gospel indicate that it was written from a very close position in time and place. Now, as I said above, John Robinson's posthumous book, The Priority of John, rebels openly against any late date. Some of us may suspect this former Bishop of Woolwich because of his damaging book, Honest to God, but he had always been a good Biblical scholar and Adrian Hastings' recent history of the last sixty years rates him head and shoulders among his fellows. I believe his last book is very convincing and it has changed my whole approach to all the Gospels.

My thoughts next move on to Acts 2:42 where we are told the first Christian converts "continued steadfastly in the apostle's teaching ...". What would be the content of this teaching? Well, if you or I had made a complete change of life because of the preaching of somebody we should want to know more about that person. We can therefore think of people sitting round the apostles and demanding as much information as possible. The Greek word for "continued steadfastly" is proskarterountes and this literally means "persisting obstinately in". Teachers will know the kind of pupil who keeps asking questions until he is satisfied. "I still don't understand" he might say and the teacher tries again to get the information over. So I imagine that in the important matter of the Lord's life, death and resurrection there would be much crossquestioning until the converts had the true picture. So an apostle would have to remember all the Master did and taught and be prepared to give accounts of it. From the beginning men like John would have to discover a teaching ministry in order to satisfy a vociferous demand. In time, no doubt, details would be written down and the outline of a Gospel take shape. This deposit of teaching material seems to have been defended with the greatest vigour, judging from the letters of St. Paul and St. John.

So when the author of the Fourth Gospel asks us to believe that he is speaking the truth (19:35, 36 and 21:24) perhaps we should accept his word. Some scholars have maintained he is protesting too much and either has something to hide or is not the original John. The history of the first generations of Christians makes such a fraud incredible. The Greek world, which since 150 BC at least had encompassed the Jews, produced great writers and among them historians. Thucydides, for example, wrote c.400 BC about the major Peloponnesians War, thinking his account would be helpful for later generations. If he is uncertain about the facts he says so, as does Herodotus before him. You are rarely in doubt whether they are reporting fact or fiction because they say so. Are we to give less credibility to writers of a Church fighting and suffering to survive?

To me John seems to be writing very close to the events. We can imagine ourselves sitting round him in the days after the resurrection and listening to his first hand account of what had happened. Robinson draws attention to a little Greek word which occurs twice in the narrative – "houtōs". Translations mostly gloss over this but in fact it can mean "just like this". So Our Lord (4:6) we are told, sits on the well, houtōs, just like this and the beloved disciple leans back on the Master's breast at the last supper, houtōs, just like this (13:25). It is stage directions like this which help us to think we are reading more than old man's reflections.

Jerusalem seems to be still standing, which it certainly was not after 70 AD. John mentions two places, Bethesda and the Praetorium (Pavement) which could obviously still be seen. They both disappeared after the destruction of 70 AD and the remains we are shown today should be taken with a pinch of salt.

Altogether John has a very accurate idea of the political and religious situation before the Romans destroyed the city. When he is talking about Jews in the Jerusalem district he rightly calls them, Judaeans. I could go on stating a case for the early writing of John but I would not wish to stop you reading John Robinson's presentation of the facts both in his Redating The New Testament and the Priority of John. I leave this section with his words; "Essentially the same point (the trial narrative) is made of his material or the typography of Jerusalem, his awareness of the geographical and psychological divisions of Palestine before the Jewish War and his use of metaphors and arguments which would have been scarcely intelligible outside a purely Jewish context in the earliest period".[12]

I have found especially convincing John's three year programme for the ministry of Jesus. This I have outlined elsewhere but a comment or two is necessary. John mentions three Passovers and shows Jesus moving up and down Palestine to keep these and other feasts. As he does so he makes friends and enemies and has a picture of the sad state of religion everywhere. So he can on his last visit weep over the city. He becomes a well-known figure in Jerusalem. He is a marked man by the authorities and has to organise his movements to keep himself out of their hands until his mission is completed. His friends include Martha, Mary and the Lazarus and the man from whom he will borrow the donkey for his final entry into the city. These acquaintances would scarcely be credible if he had only visited the city once.

In fact, all sorts of incidents fall into place if you accept a three year ministry as against the one year of the Synoptics. The latter's accounts appear, therefore, a condensation of a longer version and their style differs because of this – note the abbreviated parable form which appears to be expanded in John. The Synoptics were, after all, producing accounts without frills for the Graeco-Roman world, mostly. So local conditions would not be of great interest to such audiences. I also believe John shows more clearly the Qumran connection of the Baptist and the very beginnings of the Gospel. It must be remembered that the Dead Sea Scrolls have only been available since the last war and are still being translated. So, earlier commentaries have not been able to take such information into account. It is a tragedy that John Robinson died before he could draw out more fully the implications of this Essene community for the Christian gospel. However, I think he was able to show a way forward for this line of thought and it is possible that we may have much more to learn from this monastic community.

To understand how books saw the light of day within classical society, I find information from the Roman writer, the Younger Pliny, useful. In a letter to Caecilius he justifies his reading aloud of a work to an audience before publication. He writes "I should like to ask them (his critics) why they allow (if they do allow) readings of history whose authors aim at truth and accuracy rather than displaying their talents". He says you can avoid slips in this way and goes on, "First of all, I go through my work myself; next I read it to two or three friends and send it to others for comment. If I have any doubts about their criticisms I go over them again with one or two people and finally I read the work to a larger audience". He wrote this letter in the latter part of the first century AD. Was this the way John's Gospel emerged? If we think of his gospel being read aloud, then clarified and modified according to suggestions from his audience, we may have some clues to the place, time and authorship of the Fourth Gospel.

As a teacher I am concerned that the material for this gospel is basically that of an eye witness of the ministry of Jesus and not the ruminations of a later generation of believers. The identity of the Beloved Disciple may be in doubt but as long as we have his witness handed down to us, I am satisfied. I am also happy to accept that an editor has been at work in producing the final work because internal evidence makes this clear. If I were to return to the classroom I would consider that the Fourth Gospel was a very suitable book for study, chapter by chapter, in a senior school.

Finally if we are to have true renewal in the Church we must get right, first of all, our attitude to the Bible and especially the Gospels. If the latter seem unreliable, then the Church will sound an uncertain note and, as St. Paul notes, nobody will go out to battle. In fact the Church can only be renewed on the early Church pattern and this Vatican 11 recognised. This does not mean a resort to fundamentalism but to balanced sensible scholarship which seeks to draw out clearly the proclamation from God which was announced by Jesus. In any programme of evangelism this proclamation must be accepted by modern apostles before they can pass it on to those at present outside the Church.

A FISHY BUSINESS

If I were to start a course on the Fourth Gospel by saying that the selling of fish threw interesting light on both the author and his material, you might think I was pulling your leg. How could such a spiritual Gospel be connected with the succulent smell which greets us in most towns today? Yet if you look at the evidence from within the Gospel you will see the subject will not go away. To take a small point – in five places in John and not in the other Gospels there is a special word for cooked fish (opsarion in the Greek) as distinct to the Greek ichthus which was fresh fish straight from the sea. You are alerted here to the fact that John knew his business. We accept that some of the disciples were fishermen but fail to see the ramifications of this very important industry. So we know that John, the son of Zebedee, with his brother James belonged to a family which was in the fish business for the other Gospels tell us so (Mark 1:9). We may assume that the Zebedees were more than mere fishermen for they employed hired servants. Perhaps we might call them fish merchants. They would not be poor because the Sea of Galilee supplied the whole of Palestine (except the coast) with fish and still does. There was a plentiful supply of fish in the lake – and varied, too. It was such a flourishing industry that a salting and preserving factory had been built nearby at Tarichaeae (tarichos is the Greek word for pickling).[13]

We move on to see that it was possible for the Zebedees to supply fish to Jerusalem but they would need an agent there. Who better than John, one of the sons? We know he had a house in the city because he took Mary, the Mother of Jesus, there after the crucifixion (19:27). More about that later. If he was supervising the daily supply of fish to Jerusalem, no doubt the High priest's Palace would be on his books and we read he was known to this household (18:15). Was he known as John the Fish? So we can begin to build some kind of picture about John's background. He had a house in the city and therefore would know Jerusalem well. His Gospel shows this. It has been said even that John knows not Galilee and centres Jesus' ministry in Judaea. Not entirely true, of course, but the balance is more toward the city and in this John differs from the other Gospels. He has a close knowledge of places, Bethesda, Siloam, the Pavement etc and as I said earlier they all seem to be standing. Do we know any more about John's house in Jerusalem? When, in the next century, Christians began to return to the devastated city they found a Christian community near Mount Sion, to the south west of Jerusalem. The house of the Last Supper is today located here. Egeria who has left us a record of her pilgrimage to the Holy Land in 383 AD confirms this.[14] Certainly there seems evidence for the existence of an early Christian quarter in this district. There are also traces of an Essence community in this south west area of the city – Essenes were not confined to the monastery at Qumran beside the Dead Sea. If such a place existed in this locality we have another interesting link with the beginning of the Christian Gospel. More will be said when we deal with John Baptist's preaching in Chapter One.

As to John the evangelist's family connections, there are grounds for thinking that he was related to Jesus for according to 19.25 Our Lord's mother had a sister, Salome. She could well have been the mother of James and John, the sons of Zebedee (Priority of John p. 119). This would mean that John was a cousin of Jesus and therefore connected with the high priestly family. Hence a further reason for associating him with the High Priest's Palace. Hence also the fact that John took Our Lord's mother home with him after the crucifixion.

So we begin to find family relationships within the disciples and that was natural for the Jewish world took such matters seriously.

But if John started in Jerusalem where did he go from there? There is overwhelming evidence for his settling in Ephesus in Asia Minor. When he and his Gospel are mentioned by the early Fathers of the Church, it is always in connection with the important town of Ephesus where St. Paul left his mark. It may well be that his Gospel was written down in its final form here and this may have given rise to the idea of a later date. But I hope I have given grounds for thinking that the basic material was very close in time and place to the original ministry of Jesus. It can therefore be studied with great confidence as a true record of what Jesus said and did.

****

SEQUENCE OF EVENTS OR CHRONOLOGY IN ST. JOHN'S GOSPEL

We are looking at the years 27 – 30 AD. These can reasonably be fixed from the date of the Passover which can be traced down the years. St. John is more explicit than the Synoptics and often gives the names of places and the time of the year Jesus visited them.

27 AD   Autumn or winter, John preaches near Dead Sea where wealthy Jews are wintering.

28 AD   March? Baptism of Jesus (Chapter 1 v. 29)
April. In Cana and Capernaum (2.1). Then to
         Jerusalem for Passover.
         Cleansing of the Temple
         Passover – April 28th – May 5th. Nicodemus
May. Baptises in Judaea (3:22). Baptist arrested after preaching at Aenon.
June. Jesus leaves for Galilee. Samaritan woman at the well (4.7 ff).
October 23rd – 31st. Jerusalem for Feast of Tabernacles (5:1)
November – April. Galilee (6)

29 AD	April (green grass). Feeding of 5,000 (Before Passover)
	May – September. North Palestine and Galilee (6:35)
	October 15th. Feast of Tabernacles again (7)
	November – December. Judaea and Peraea (10:22 – 40)
	December 20 – 27. Feast of Dedication in Jerusalem
30 AD	January – February. Bethany beyond Jordan (11:54) Note 11:47
	Jesus tried in absence?
	February. Bethany near Jerusalem and Ephraim
	April 2 – 6. Bethany near Jerusalem
	April 7th. Crucifixion

THE PEOPLE FOR WHOM JOHN WROTE

If you take the view that John wrote in old age in Ephesus in Asia Minor, as I was taught before the war, you may well conclude that his readers or hearers were Christians in a developing and growing Church outside Palestine.

But if we take the line that John's material, at any rate, is early then we will have to think again about the destination of his Gospel. The first three Gospels have been the subject of much speculation about their purpose. John Robinson notes in an essay "In the Synoptic Gospels the centre of the stage is also occupied by the Jews. But we are conscious always of the Gentiles pressing in on the wings".[15] Indeed I learnt very early that Mark was written and constructed for people in Rome. Their interest in the Gentiles, the very shape of their works with material falling neatly into two halves, the first in Galilee and the second in Judaea indicates that their audience might only be interested in a concise account of the teaching and works of Jesus.

But John is different. His handling of the geography and the chronology of the Gospel indicates he is writing for people who are interested in those subjects. John's Gospel also is remarkable for the fact that the Gentiles are not mentioned. The only foreigner who gets a mention is Pilate but he could scarcely fail to get this through his role in the final trial of Jesus. None of the references to Gentiles which we find in the Synoptics are in John. True he speaks about the world but this means all created beings. It is a cosmic reference. Jesus is the true light who "enlightens every man who comes into the world". Then there is the great universalistic saying, "If I am lifted up I will draw all men unto me". This is a deeper sentiment than a mission to the Gentiles. The world here is not just non-Jews but all people, both Jew and otherwise. The contrast in this Gospel is not between Jew and Gentile but between light and darkness. The only true Jewish faith is one which recognises Jesus as the Messiah. This may mean taking an entirely new view of Jewishness and involves a being born again as Jesus said to Nicodemus who did not understand him.

11

In fact John's Gospel is very rooted in Palestine and a political situation which existed before the fall of Jerusalem. Yet in several places we can find an intense anti-Jewish attitude. The Jews can be seen as villains of the piece. They are responsible for delivering Jesus up to the Romans; they hound Jesus for most of his ministry and try to stone him on several occasions.

But there were other Jews living in Palestine apart from this antagonistic party and they are possibly referred to by the words "the common people". They are probably referred to in John 7:49, "This people who know not the law are accursed". This set of people seem to have been divided into Aramaic-speaking Jews and Greek speaking Jews. The latter would have been born abroad in the Dispersion and would have been brought up to speak only Greek. They read the Scriptures in this language and had their own synagogues. They may well have lived lightly to Jewish festivals and customs. We find in Acts 6:1 that there was a disagreement between the Grecians and Hebrews. As a result, deacons were appointed, of which one was Stephen. His martyrdom might have inspired more Hellenist Jews to join the Church and so we would have a growing group which would need to have its own account of the ministry of Jesus. John Robinson suggests that John wrote for these people and if the Gospel is re-read in the light of this suggestion, light is thrown on certain texts. They might need to have certain customs described (2:6 and 6:4); and the disgust and contempt behind 7:35 – "does he intend to go to the Dispersion and teach the Greeks") might be explained. Also we have light on Jesus' insistence that there will be one flock under one shepherd. This does not mean, as we use it, just a general unity but the healing of the divisions within Judaism. This is brought out in the saying of Caiaphas 11:51. John writes, "he did not say this of his own accord but being high priest that year he prophesied that Jesus should die for the nation and not for the nation only, but to gather into one the children of God who are scattered abroad". The 'nation' here would be inner circle Jews in Jerusalem and the 'children of God scattered abroad' might be the Greeks Jews.

If John was writing for this set of Greek Jews living in Palestine, he could report Jesus as using images of himself from the Old Testament – Manna, Light, Shepherd, Vine.

If we reckon up such evidence, we may well conclude that John wrote not for faraway people in Asia Minor but for a very local audience in Palestine itself and in the early days of the expanding Christian Church.

A NOTE ON SEEING JESUS IN THE WRITINGS OF ST. JOHN

I am indebted to John Robinson for listing the ways Jesus can be seen in the Gospel. In his book The Priority of John he shows there are four ways people looked at Jesus in the days of his earthly ministry. I have adapted these ideas because I think it helps us to understand the mind of the evangelist as he records the details of Our Lord's life.

1. Jesus could be seen at a purely human level. This is the way of the unbelieving or uncomprehending Jews. They saw without believing or understanding the relationship of Jesus to God. He was regarded as just another human being but mad, bad and a deceiver of the people.

2. He could be seen with the eyes of faith. Some people noted the way Jesus worked and taught and recognised that God was at work in him. They believed through seeing – the Samaritan woman and her neighbours, the officer of Herod's household etc. So the Church must for ever look behind the ministry of Jesus to God the Father who speaks to us through him. So the works and words of Our Lord must be proclaimed in every generation so that all men may have the opportunity of believing in the same way.

3. Having seen that God the Father was with Jesus, people could look back at Gospel events and re-interpret every action of Jesus. His ministry can be seen in greater depth. This new insight will have been sharpened by the fact of the Resurrection.

So we should realise that John writes from *this* side of the Resurrection and so can see every word and deed of Jesus in the days of his earthly ministry as being shot through with risen glory. The life of Our Lord can be entered in greater depth. No longer do we say of him, This is the Christ, but that we can see the Father in the Son – he is the Word (Logos).

So a meaning not perceived at the time can be drawn out of every incident. This is a special feature of John's Gospel.

It will be realised that we have a different composition from one where events are recorded as they happened – in diary form perhaps.

4. But from both the Gospels and the Letters of St. John we can see he was aware of the danger of belief in Jesus without a historical background. Read the opening verses of 1 John and 2 John 7 – 9. The Gospel, too, insists on the importance of the 'fleshly' fact of the Incarnation and the earthly life which flowed from it. There is no competition between the flesh and the spirit, between history and theology. They supplement each other. Chapter 19:35 foll sets out this fact clearly.

This is a lesson for us today when some scholars are devaluing the integrity of history so that all that is left is a commitment to an idea of Jesus. The charismatic movement, too, has often lost the balance between the spiritual and the historical so that all that is left is an emotional attachment to the Lord. John recalls us to the concrete facts of Jesus' sojourn on earth and the disciplined Christian life which must flow from it for all disciples.

THE TEXT

Whether you conclude John's Gospel was written early or late, the hand of an editor is clearly visible. If we think of the main body of material as given orally in the early days of the Church and later written down we may have some answer to the argument about the date of the Gospel. As I have indicated earlier I am convinced that John is very close to the original events of the Lord's ministry and is more than an old man's meditation. But both the beginning and the end of the Gospel seem to be later additions. If we think of John narrating what he knew about Jesus to those who had recently been converted, we have difficulty in accepting the rather florid, theological prologue as his opening remarks. It is more likely that he would begin with John the Baptist.

John Robinson likens the prologue (1:1 – 19) to a porch of a house, designed and executed by the same architect but in a grander and more elevated style and this seems a good description.

Chapter 21 also seems to have been added later and stands as an Epilogue. Brevard Charles thinks it gives a clue to how the whole Gospel is rendered. He writes, "in short the chapter offers an excellent example of canonical shaping which reflects on issues addressing the mission of the Church in future generations, indeed from the resurrection to the return of Christ."[16] In other words the Gospel is shaped to ensure the handing on of the original divine revelation. The editor wishes to shape the faith of future generations by a faithful account of what happened in the life of Jesus. The Gospel was meant to create faith in the future not describe reactions of those who had received it already. So the last chapter is not another attempt to rouse faith in the risen Christ but rather how the disciples were to minister to the world in the light of the resurrection. It shows how later generations should respond to the new life they have received. You might say we have here something of the mechanics of mission. This will be dealt with when we reach the last chapter.

CHAPTER ONE

FROM ETERNITY TO HERE

The Prologue (verses 1 – 18). If we think this Gospel started with one of the disciples satisfying the early converts with more information about the life and work of Jesus, then the opening verses must be a problem. As I said above it was more likely that the narrator would start with such words as "It all started with John the Baptist". At some time therefore this most beautiful opening must have been added. R.E. Brown says "If John has been described as the pearl of great price among the New Testament writings, then one may say that the Prologue is the pearl within this Gospel". He goes on to call it a hymn phrased in words which could appeal to a Greek audience. Yet we do not need to turn to Greek philosophy to find the inspiration for this wonderful piece of writing.

1. *In the beginning was the word.* This sophisticated opening has led some to think that it was composed at the end of the first century after the style of the Greek philosopher, Philo. Scholars have mentioned other sources from the same period but this background is unnecessary. There had been Greek influence in Palestine for nearly two hundred years before Christ so if a Greek origin to these opening verses is sought there is no need to look for a late date. In fact we need to look little further than the Old Testament – Genesis 1 and Proverbs 8. The latter is part of Jewish Wisdom literature where wisdom is personified.

5. *The light shines in darkness but the darkness does not understand.* More significant is this contrast between light and darkness because a confrontation between light and darkness is a subject of the Dead Sea scrolls. Later in this chapter we shall note the possible link between the Qumran community and John the Baptist. Only in the last thirty years have we been in a position to consider this connection. This has happened through the discovery and translation of the scrolls.

7. *This man came for a witness.* In this word 'witness' we find the reason for John's Gospel. It is all about witnessing to the word who became flesh and later this witness will be supported by certain signs or miracles such as the turning of water into wine and the curing of sick people. The whole gospel throbs with excitement that God has revealed himself through his Son in such a way that he who seen the Son has seen the Father also. Since then it has been the duty of the Church in every age to pass on that revelation or proclamation about God's will for his people. The Greek word for such a proclamation is kerugma.

And the word was made flesh. These words are at the very heart of the Church's message. This unique event has occupied the minds of every generation of Christian believers. Greek and Latin scholars have tried to fathom the theological niceties of the Incarnation and put it into simple language. They have mostly failed and some have fallen into heresy when they emphasised either the divine or the human side of Jesus' nature at the expense of the other. The taking of flesh by the son of God is a mystery. "Mystery" is a specialist word which needs to be spelt out to lay people. It is a secret thing, known only to God; which is part of his plan for creation and has to be worked out in a history not yet ended. S. Paul suggests an inexpressible reality which gives us a mere glimpse into the infinite. Christians have to accept the way God works in his becoming man for our salvation. S. Athanasius tussled with this mystery as much as most and writes: "The Word took this course of action so that he could take on himself what was ours, offer it in sacrifice, then do away with it altogether, and then clothe us in what was his, as he inspired the Apostle to say: 'this perishable nature must put on the imperishable and this mortal must put on immortality'. "The more practical Western Catholic might well be satisfied with that summary and not probe any deeper. We have had too much unwise speculation about the person of Christ over the last 150 years and the result has often been to reduce him to the level of just another religious leader. This is not John's teaching.

The Incarnation is the greatest mystery; accept that and all other mysteries fall into place – how Our Lord can come to us in Communion, how the Eucharist can be an offering of man to God and an approach of God to us through the same Jesus, how miracles are possible, how other sacraments work and so on.

And dwelt among us. The visit of the Son of God to our world was no brief affair, like the descending of the Greek and Roman gods and goddesses. He shared our life. The Greek word for 'dwelt' is literally 'pitched his tent among us'. This term would be familiar to the Jews for they remembered the time when their forefathers lived in tents during their trek through the desert under Moses. Many thought this was the high point of their history. More comfortable life in Palestine had lowered their standards and they needed to be rescued from this. So the Son of God entered the pilgrimage of everyman, to get him moving on his way to God again.

The Son of God was clothed with our flesh, was incarnate. There was a short time in history when one man could look at his neighbour and see the human face of God, could hear God speaking in his own vocabulary. God had something to say to us and spoke his message within daily life, through an encounter of man to man. Some accepted the message, changed their lives and passed the information to others. This encounter has been caught and held for us in the Gospels.

If the Gospel of John contains any reflections or meditation on the life of Jesus, it can be found in the Prologue. Perhaps this is a later hand at work which has puzzled scholars and led them to think that the whole Gospel should not be taken as serious history. But very quickly we reach a straightforward clear narrative of events which have all the signs of being that of a close eye witness.

19 – 34 With the words *'this is the testimony of John'* we enter the field of sheer history. You can hear the Gospel writer saying to those who sought information after the Resurrection, "of course, it all began with John the Baptist" and he would begin to pour out his amazing story.

The gospel truly started with the Baptist, much more than most have realised, I believe.

28. *These things took place at Bethany beyond Jordan.* Thanks to pilgrim tradition we can locate this place, (not to be confused with the Bethany on the edge of Jerusalem). It was east of the river Jordan and now in the country of Jordan. On the west side of the Jordan stands Jericho (now Israel). The river was fordable at this spot and suitable for baptisms. A short distance downstream the river flows into the Dead Sea. It is very hot in this part of the world which is a mile below sea level. In the summer the heat and the evaporating chemicals of the Dead Sea make it a very unpleasant place to live in. But in the winter from November to about March it is pleasantly warm and some Jerusalem inhabitants would winter there. Leisure amenities had been built. Josephus writes, "the climate is so mild that the inhabitants wear linen when snow is falling throughout the rest of Judaea".[17] So John would have an audience for his preaching during the winter months. The hot months would not have been suitable for such activity.

Of greater interest is the Qumran community which was situated not far from the main Dead Sea beach. Recent excavations have given us a good idea of the life which went on there and the finding of the Dead Sea scrolls in 1947 enable us to understand the teaching of the community. Since there are indications that John Baptist and his followers had connections here, it is necessary to look more closely at this Qumran or Essene monastery.

It was situated near the northern edge of the Dead Sea, about 15 miles from the capital, Jerusalem. The road winds steeply downward from the city which is set on Mount Sion. So it was near enough to be under the scrutiny of the Jerusalem authorities. The community had small offshoots throughout Palestine, including a possible one in the capital. It had been founded about 100 BC by religious Jews who had become disillusioned with the ecclesiastical politics of the time. They had isolated themselves to await the coming of the Messiah, the Teacher of Righteousness. They had a rigorous daily routine of prayer, ceremonial purifying with water, a common meal and manual craft among which was the copying and writing of holy books. They held property in common and did not practise marriage although they could adopt children. A candidate was not admitted before he had completed three years of probation. They wore white robes. The sect was composed of the priestly class and laity and was strictly governed. The Dead Sea scrolls which are still being translated give great detail about their teaching.

Of interest to us is the teaching that by their life and discipline and through an inner group dedicated to perfection, the community will become agents of God's atoning work and judgment ("to make atonement for the guilt of transgression and sinful infidelity" – I QS 9:4). Also they believed that their way of life with its emphasis on perfection and purification by water was provisional until a new outpouring of the Holy Spirit took place. Here we begin to find characteristic themes of John Baptist's preaching – refining, cleansing, water and Holy Spirit. This leads to the thought that the Baptist had been a member of this community, see Luke 1: 80. If so, he would have been a priestly member if we remember his family connection. The monastery seems to have been destroyed by an earthquake in 31 BC and only revived in the reign of Archelaus (4 BC – 6 AD). The rebuilding of this community might have attracted young men who wanted an alternative to the official religion. Maybe John thought the kingdom of God was closer than his fellows believed and he left to be its herald.

So with the help of the recently discovered Scrolls we can begin to build a base for understanding further the gospel Jesus preached. For the evangelist, John, the curtain rises in the winter months, on an area near the Dead Sea where the Baptist, supported by a few followers, is attracting crowds by his preaching of an imminent intervention by God into human affairs. Into this scene came Jesus and associated himself with his cousin's message. Who knows what had gone on in the family circle of Mary, Joseph, Zachariah and Elizabeth, Jesus and John, which inspired the remark, Behold the Lamb of God? Note that the Gospel starts with a proclamation from the Baptist that the son of God had come into the world. Jesus accepts John's witness, completing and unfolding God's message for the world in the rest of the Gospel. This good news, however, owed much to the conditions of the time and flowed from a situation which we find round the Dead Sea. The ministry of Jesus starts here and not at Galilee.

19. Priests and Levites whose work was in the Temple made the fairly short journey down from Jerusalem. Since John was from a priestly family they would naturally want to check on what he was doing.

21. *I am not the Christ.* John's presentation of the Baptist is not very different from the Synoptics. If he was preaching over a number of weeks, reporting of events was bound to vary.

23. *Make straight the way of the Lord.* Compare the Manual of Discipline at Qumran: "Now when these things (a future state of perfection) come to pass in Israel to the community, according to these rules, they will separate themselves from the midst of the habitation of perverse men, to go into the wilderness to clear a way (of the Lord), as it is written:
In the wilderness clear the way of the Lord;
Level in the desert a highway for our God."

18

When such an ideal state was reached and an inner group had been purified from sin, they will march into the wilderness and the final battle with the sons of darkness will begin. So it is possible for us to see in retrospect that this perfect state had been reached in one man, Jesus. Now the battle between good and evil can begin, and did. John's Gospel shows clearly this contrast between light and darkness.

29. *There is the Lamb of God.* No satisfactory parallel is found at Qumran but this might belong to a general apocalyptic tradition. Certainly there was a redemptive element in the community's teaching – "to atone for all those who dedicate themselves for holiness in 'Aaron" IQS 5:5. We might remember Isaiah's teaching about the suffering servant and the sheep led to the slaughter. We have in fact a picture of a sect who had not just withdrawn from public life to escape a coming judgment but aimed at creating a special purified remnant. This might well have compelled Our Lord to identify with it. But there is also found in the Scrolls the teaching that this faithful remnant might be embodied in one man. "At that time God will purify by his truth all the deeds of a man ... and he will sprinkle upon him the Spirit of truth as purifying water". I QS 4:20.

32. *I saw the Spirit coming down from heaven.* As we have seen the Qumran community taught this coming of the Holy Spirit when the time was ripe.

John's Gospel gives us more information than the Synoptics about the very beginnings of Jesus' message. No matter how great the teacher, there has to be some kind of local situation and language to which he can appeal. A good teacher goes from the known to the unknown. We might ask if Jesus started by being a follower of the Baptist. It could explain the words in v.27 *He who comes after me* – which can be translated as easily, "there is a man in my following". The Synoptics do not lead us to think that Jesus has any continuing association with John. It would be natural for the early Church to fade the Baptist out of the Gospel.

Somehow John's reporting of the scene near the Jordan seems fresh and convincing. He shows also how the first disciples came from the Baptist's followers – they were also present when he baptised Jesus and drew attention to him. We do not find any friction in the changing of loyalties. Indeed if John recognised Jesus as the expected Messiah he could not have resented the new leadership. So we come now to the signing on of the first disciples.

37. *The two disciples heard John say this and followed Jesus.* They were named as Andrew and Simon – note Andrew first. The transfer of loyalty seems to happen naturally. John identifies the Messiah and Andrew, then Simon Peter took the hint. They were followed by Philip and Nathaniel. There is no mention of John but the Greek in verse 41 would stand the inclusion of another two. So we get a nucleus of five – Andrew, Peter, James, John and Philip to be

followed by Nathaniel. See C.K. Barrett, The Gospel According to John pp. 181 and 182 on these verses.

The Synoptic account of the first disciples takes place at Galilee and we have no knowledge of their religious background. It would seem that Jesus started from scratch with them. But if we accept John's account we can know that Jesus and his disciples started with the common belief that a small group, living dedicated lives, could be agents in the coming of God's kingdom. This is a pattern we need to follow today.

John makes no mention of the forty days in the wilderness but transports us immediately to Cana. However, it should be noted that this was a considerable journey which could take several days.

CHAPTER TWO

NORTH AND SOUTH

This is a short chapter with two main subjects, the wedding at Cana in Galilee and the cleansing of the temple.

1. *On the third day.* This can scarcely follow on from the first chapter because it was a long journey from the Dead Sea area to Northern Palestine, at least 60 miles as the crow flies. John could be following on from an incident not mentioned, or it could be the third day of the week which was Tuesday. One commentator notes that this was considered a lucky day for weddings in Bible times, just as Saturday is a popular day now.

4. *What have I to do with thee, or, Your concern, Mother, is not mine (NEB).* This is not necessarily rude. It indicates a reluctance to take any decisive action. If this was Our Lord's first miracle we can understand the hesitation.

9. *Water into wine.* This miracle can be seen alongside the feeding of the 5,000 etc. We may find it difficult to understand. Healing miracles are one thing and can be envisaged but nature miracles pose a problem. We must not ask how Jesus did them because that would be treating him as a magician. We can never know but trust the Gospel writer who obviously believed something important had happened. But apart from a brief mention of Cana "where he turned water into wine" (4:45) the incident is not mentioned again and played no significant part in the Gospel overall.

I find helpful C.S. Lewis' remark in his book, Miracles. "Every year, as part of the natural order, God makes wine. He does so by creating vegetable organism that can turn water, soil, and sunlight into a juice which will, under proper conditions, become wine. Thus, in a certain sense, he constantly turns water into wine for wine, like all drinks, is but water modified. Once and in one year only, God, now incarnate, short circuits the process – makes water into wine in a few moments."[18] We do well to leave it there.

Commentators chiefly discuss the symbolism of the incident – the water of the old Jewish religion turned into the richer Christian faith.

12. Jesus now goes to Capernaum, a short distance away, beside the Sea of Galilee. Considerable excavation has been done here in recent years and a very ancient synagogue brought to light, part of which might well have belonged to Jesus' day. Some scholars think that Jesus and his mother moved here from Nazareth – after Joseph died? Capernaum was an important fishing port and trading centre in Our Lord's day.

13. *The time of the Jewish Passover.* This would be in April. So Jesus, having gone north from the Dead Sea, now makes the journey south, taking several days.

24. *Drove them out of the temple.* The words of Malachi might be remembered: "Suddenly, the Lord whom you seek will come to his temple .... he will purify the Levites and cleanse them like gold and silver".

Today's visitor to the Holy Land will know that the holy places have been commercialised. He is besieged by men wanting to sell souvenirs. It seems it was little different in Our Lord's day only here traders had cashed in on people's piety and sold sacrificial items at inflated prices. Jesus drove them out and the words of the Psalmist came to mind, "the zeal of thine house hath eaten me up".

18. The Jews challenged Jesus. They ask for a sign of his authority for taking such drastic action. Jesus made a remark which at his trial was vaguely remembered, that if the Temple were destroyed he could rebuild it in three days. With hindsight John saw this as a prophecy of the resurrection.

20. *It has taken forty six years to build this temple, the Jews reply.* Here is an important clue to the date of the present events. We know Herod started this rebuilding 20 – 19 BC. Forty six years on would bring us to 27 – 28 AD and this fits in well with other evidence we have.

22. *After his resurrection the disciples remembered ...* John is being perfectly honest. When Jesus first spoke these words the disciples did not understand. Perhaps they were even embarrassed by them and thought the authorities were being unnecessarily provoked. They might well have attributed the hostility which pursued Jesus during his visits to Jerusalem later to this remark. The Temple was more than a building. It was the very centre of the Jewish faith and

synagogues were built pointing in that direction. So a threat to destroy it would be taken very seriously.

But when John is narrating the Gospel to the first Christians after Pentecost he sees this saying of Jesus in its true light. Matters the disciples did not understand during their master's earthly ministry became flooded with the radiance of the resurrection. So we can begin to understand the development of this Gospel writer. First we have the eye witness with limited vision. I mean, he had an undeveloped faith and did not see from the beginning the full implication of Jesus. He saw him not with an unworldly dimension but at best as a prophet who could work signs or miracles. We find in several places in the four Gospels that Jesus was sometimes exasperated by the thickheadness of his disciples. Even after his resurrection he chided the disciples on the way to Emmaus with stupidity and dull minds. But the coming of the Holy Spirit at Pentecost changed all that and the teachers of the early converts to the Faith could interpret the whole Gospel in the light of the resurrection. It gave the words and events a deeper and inexhaustible meaning. As we shall see in the incident of the Samaritan woman at the well, the promise of Jesus to give living water is not understood. But John from this side of the resurrection knows that the risen Lord can satisfy the deepest spiritual thirst. We today with St. John may draw infinite value from Our Lord's words and deeds if we see them in the light of the resurrection.

We have a problem with John's account of the incident of the cleansing of the Temple because the Synoptics place it at the end of Jesus' ministry, just before the Passion. Indeed it can be read as a prime cause of his arrest.

Who is right? In this we need to understand that the first three Gospels pack the ministry into one year only and record one visit only of Jesus to Jerusalem, just before his arrest and trial. John, however, gives us a three year ministry with Our Lord visiting Jerusalem regularly. Only if we accept John's time scale can we explain the contacts of Jesus there and his familiarity with what is going on in the city. John, too, might have seen this cleansing of the Temple as a decisive event but early in the ministry – a distant cause of his trial and execution. We find in the Gospels and especially in John an early antagonism to Jesus and even attempts to arrest and stone him (John 7:1). This could be explained by the abrasive protest in the Temple at the beginning of the ministry.

However, if it offended some, it made a favourable impression on some Jewish laymen who rallied round him and supported him.

24. *Jesus did not entrust himself to them ... he knew what was in man.* Lightfoot says of these verses, "The Lord himself was able to assess the interest thus aroused at its true value and did not seek to build on it; himself the word become flesh and therefore the source of life and light he had immediate knowledge of the heart

of every man".[19] He goes on to note that those who come into contact with the Lord, ipso facto come into judgment – they are divided into those who believe and those who do not.

The theme of manifestation or revelation is central to John's Gospel as also is the act of witnessing. The disciples see his power at the wedding feast and believe, at least partially. Next we move to Jerusalem where Jesus again shows his authority and a number believe although Jesus does not take their commitment too seriously. This is followed by the witness to Nicodemus and then a further witnessing from the Baptist. Then an ordinary citizen, a woman in Samaria, next becomes a pupil of Jesus' revelation. All this should remind us that witnessing is the chief duty of a Christian in any age. As Nicodemus and then the Samaritan woman questioned him intelligently, so we, too, have to probe the deepest mysteries of our Faith.

CHAPTER THREE

NICODEMUS

The protest of Jesus in the Temple made him enemies among the Jewish authorities, not only because an unqualified teacher had interfered with their own department but because it threatened the delicate situation in Roman-occupied Palestine. The Romans could intervene fiercely if the stability of the country was threatened. There had been a number of incidents by Jewish hotheads who wanted the Romans out. The situation was similar to the present state of affairs in Israel where Jews try to keep under control Palestinian communities. Jesus could be seen as one trying to rock the boat and becomes a marked man. Throughout this Gospel there are clues that the Jews in authority would like him out of the way (5:16; 7:1; 8:59; 10:32; 11:7/53).

But some were impressed by Jesus' forthright action and one of them, under cover of darkness, comes to find out more. This is the best situation for a teacher, when somebody asks for information. The need for knowledge is the best starting point in any branch of education. Lay apostles today should be ready to deal with inquirers about religion.

2. *Nobody can do these signs.* So far John has only reported two 'signs' – water into wine and the cleansing of the Temple. Perhaps there are others not reported. The incident at Cana was unlikely to have reached Nicodemus' ears in Jerusalem. His opening approach was very much in the Middle Eastern style – polite, courteous and undemanding. Note Nicodemus accepts Jesus as a teacher whereas in 7:15 he is called unlearned. But the greeting is not so generous as it seems. Nicodemus is saying that God is no less with Jesus than he was with Old Testament prophets.

3. *Unless a man has been born over again.* Jesus injects an edge into the conversation which might have gently drifted on. 'Again' might be translated 'from above'.

5. *Born from water and the Spirit.* Nicodemus does not understand this remark and so Jesus mentions the Qumran teaching on the subject. Rabbis in Judaea could scarcely be ignorant of Essene doctrine for it was almost on their doorstep.

8. *The Spirit blows where it will.* You can never tell when inspiration from God will strike you. It is like a breeze which can suddenly rustle the leaves of an olive tree. This can happen without warning even on the hottest day.

9. *How can this be?* Nicodemus is out of his depth. This is different language from simply living under the Law where clever debating only was necessary. Yet Jesus has spoken only of everyday examples which can be seen around us . Jesus is using a parable and he is not understood (compare, Mark 4:13).

14. *This Son of Man must be lifted up as the serpent.* Jesus reveals heavenly things but they are rejected. This rejection will finally lead to the Cross. Throughout John's Gospel the shadow of the cross is never far away. For the lifting up of the serpent see Numbers 21:4 – 9. The serpents themselves did not heal the bites but were the symbol of God at work. See Wisdom 16:6 fol. According to Jewish tradition the uplifted serpents drew the hearts of Israel to God for their salvation. So the uplifted Jesus would draw all men to himself.

16. *God so loved the world that he gave.* Temple says that this is the heart of the Gospel. It is not 'God is love' because, although this is a precious truth it says nothing about how that love was shown in the sending of Jesus. The opening words of the Benedictus should be placed alongside this saying – "Blessed be the Lord God of Israel for he has visited and redeemed his people". So we are not speaking of a general divine power but of somebody who acts in history.

19. *This is the judgment.* The Greek word used is *krisis* which means 'that which separates'. People are divided into two parties, those who accept the light which Jesus brought into the world and those who do not. Men are judged by their reaction to the work and person of Jesus (Barrett). So you may say the judgment takes place in this world by the way we decide for or against our Lord. This should be a very sobering thought for us all.

That light has come into the world. Here we touch on the Qumran teaching about the battle between light and darkness. The armies of the Prince of Darkness are composed of those who love evil.

This conversation with Nicodemus looks untidy and yet it is the way a religious argument develops with several ideas thrown out. But Jesus brings the

24

encounter round to the central point of God's saving work. This is a lesson for all who deal with questions from outside the Church. We do not know if Nicodemus was convinced but we find him in 7:50 as an ally of Jesus when the authorities were debating action against him. In 19:39 Nicodemus helps with the burial of Jesus. Sometimes people do not at first show any definite signs of being influenced by Christian instruction and then the penny drops and they align themselves with the Church. For anybody who has had to teach in the sidelines of the Church, the Nicodemus incident rings very true.

22. The action now switches to a further witness of John the Baptist. He has moved north along the Jordan valley to a place called *Aenon* which means 'Springs'. It has been suggested that the Samaritans used the place as a retreat from summer heat. So we might think of John as preaching to another holiday crowd. Salim is in north Samaria and no distance from Jacob's well at Sychar where we next find our Lord. John only has this Baptist material. Perhaps it was inserted for the benefit of those who had continued as his disciples after his death. It was meant to show that there was no reason for perpetuating the sect for there was no division between Jesus and the Baptist. On the contrary, spiritual harm would happen if the witness of Jesus was rejected.

CHAPTER FOUR

THE WOMAN AT JACOB'S WELL AND THE HEALING AT CANA

John's narrative moves smoothly and logically forward. The focus in the south of the country, Judaea, turns upon Jesus instead of the Baptist. To avoid the attentions of the Pharisees who resisted any attempts upon their authority Jesus travels north. There now follows a kind of hide and seek between him and the Jewish authorities which is not finally ended until his arrest in Gethsemane. Jesus has work to do and must not be stopped prematurely. By the time he is arrested he has completed his mission.

There were two ways north, along the Jordan valley (the shorter) and through the centre of the country. Jesus chose the latter – to escape clashing with the Baptist who was preaching near the Jordan?

Vv 6 – 43. Jesus and the Samaritan woman at Jacob's well.

The way this incident is understood will depend on whether an early or late date for the Gospel is taken. If it is concluded that it was written at the end of the first century there is a case for saying that historical accuracy takes second place to an editor's manipulation. Importance is given in the latter case to the

Church's reflection on events rather than to a straightforward remembered account.

Here we might pay attention to R.E. Brown who says, "the mise en scene (or setting) is one of the most detailed in John and the evangelist betrays a knowledge of local colour and Samaritan beliefs that is impressive. We may mention: the well at the foot of Gerizim: the question of legal purity in v.9: the spirited defence of the patriarchal well in v.12: the Samaritan belief in Gerizim and the prophet-like Moses". He goes on "Either we are dealing with a master of fiction or else the stories have a basis of fact".[20] Here some words of C.S. Lewis on St. John's Gospel in a lecture may further help here. Talking about this incident at Jacob's Well and other parts of the narrative, he says, "I have been reading poems, romances, vision-literature, legends, myths all my life. I know what they are like. I know that not one of them is like this. Of this next there are only two possible views. Either this is reportage – though it may contain some errors – pretty close up to the facts; nearly as close as Boswell. Or else, some unknown writer in the second century, without known predecessors or successors, suddenly anticipated the whole technique of modern, novelistic, realistic narrative. If it is untrue it must be narrative of that kind. The reader who doesn't see this has simply not learned to read."[21]

An early date for this gospel would not give so much scope for an author's literary sophistications and would aim at just giving the facts. So what appears to be a variation on the original theme of a simple encounter beside the well with Jesus' remarks (vv21 ff) going off at a tangent might well show how the conversation actually went. We noted in the Nicodemus episode that religious discussions often straggle unpredictably.

It has been assumed that we have a tête-à-tête between Jesus and the woman but this was very unlikely at such a public spot – the only water supply for the town. We are told the disciples had gone away to get food but did the writer remain to keep Jesus company? Samaria was hostile soil for a single Jew.

v.6 No matter how landscapes change, wells mostly survive and today it is possible to visit Jacob's Well (the political situation permitting) and enjoy the beautiful clear water. *Jesus tired after his journey sat down by the well.* This translation from the Greek omits a small word 'houtōs' which can easily be rendered 'in this way' or 'just like this'. Perhaps we have a clue here about how the Gospel came into being – John narrated with stage directions, 'he sat down just like this' and somebody wrote it down.

V.9 You a Jew ask a drink of me, a Samaritan. There was a long history behind the surprise that a Jew could actually make such an approach. Samaritans were regarded by Jews as a mixed breed since they had intermarried with foreigners after the Assyrian invasion in about 700 BC. They had also tried to prevent the rebuilding of Jerusalem when people from the southern kingdom returned from

26

exile in Babylon in the 5th century BC. More than this, the Samaritans, banned from the Temple in Jerusalem at that time, had set up their own place of sacrifice on Mount Gerizim in Samaria and so the split was complete. It is ironic that the Temple in Jerusalem was destroyed by the Romans in 70 AD but Gerizim survived and a diminishing number of Samaritans still sacrifice there.

V.10 He would have given you living water. The conversation moves quickly to deeper things. We know from the Nicodemus incident that Jesus is not interested in small talk but wants to provoke serious thought. His mission is too important to be lost in trivialities. The idea of flowing or living water appears in the Old Testament, indicating the action of God in giving spiritual life.

John is writing from this side of the Resurrection and understands exactly that Jesus could offer this divine gift. The woman, of course, does not have this dimension and keeps the conversation at a practical level. How good to have a continual supply of water! She would not have the chore of going to the well each day.

16 – 19. Some think Jesus used an exceptional power of divination which enabled him to see into this woman's life. But might he not have picked up some gossip from the comings and goings at the well. "Here comes *that* woman. I wonder how she is getting on with her latest!" Anyway the woman understands she is dealing with an exceptional person and throws out a question which had continually nagged at Samaritans – who had the right centre for sacrifice and worship, Samaritans or Jews? Jesus notes the Samaritan situation is not satisfactory – breaking away from a main body weakens religious faith. When salvation comes it will be from the mainstream of the Jewish faith. Indeed it is already here and both Jerusalem and Gerizim will be irrelevant. This leads on to another familiar theme of the Messiah which Jew and Samaritan shared. Then comes the punch line – "I, who am speaking to you, am the Christ you speak of".

The woman does not take this in fully but nevertheless knows that here is a special person and runs with the news into the town.

31. The disciples return with food but Jesus says he already has other meat and drink. They do not understand, just as the woman had not understood the reference to living water.

35 ff. Jesus says you normally allow four months between sowing and reaping on the land but in the matter of preaching the word of God, the gap may be shorter, as it is here. This was because others had been at work, laying a foundation. No doubt Jesus is speaking about the Baptist who at that time was preaching not far away at Salim. You can see Jacob's Well from Salim or Aenon. The Baptist had stirred people up and so paved the way for Jesus' visit.

The writer shows how true this is – the Samaritans persuade Jesus to stay for two days, with good effect.

43. Jesus completes his journey to Galilee and despite pessimism about his standing there, is given a good welcome because of the impact he had made at the Passover in Jerusalem – the country boy had made good in the big city!

46 – end. **Return to Cana.** This would seem to be a parallel with the cure described in the Synoptics of the centurion's son. But there is an important difference. In John the officer belongs to Herod's entourage and is not a Gentile. In fact, the only non-Jew mentioned in John is Pilate. This raises a question about the destination of this Gospel. Robinson in an essay suggested it was directed neither at traditional Jews nor to Gentiles but to Jews of the Greek Dispersion (Diaspora) who could be found in Palestine and outside. If we pursue this idea it could take us to the very early days of the Church when some Jews were asking for more information about Jesus and John set about providing the material. As we have seen there is evidence that the Gospel started by being given orally (houtōs v. 6).

Before we leave this chapter we might note that there are lessons to be learnt for the promotion of the Gospel today.

1. We should not hesitate to reach out to people who might need us
2. We should only do this if we have something important to offer
3. We should deal with others in a way which gains their trust and friendship
4. Through such an adventure of contacting others we might find ourselves drawn into an area of life which had been closed before. We may be regarded as having an ingredient of life which they lack and we must not disappoint them.

CHAPTER FIVE

THE SOUTH AGAIN

Jesus now travels south again for a feast in Jerusalem. If we follow John's chronology, this could be in October when the Feast of Tabernacles was celebrated. Pentecost in May/June was too early and the Dedication festival in midwinter is unlikely because it would be too cold for the sick to lie about in the open.

Tabernacles brought to mind the time when the Israelites had lived in tents in the wilderness. It was a reminder of the bad old days from which God had saved them. It also celebrated the final ingathering of the harvest.

2. Bethesda. Today's pilgrim to Jerusalem is shown a colonnade round two

pools but this is unlikely to have been the scene of the reported 'sign'. The columns now seen are part of the Byzantine church and the pools would not have been suitable as a place of healing. However, in the area which Josephus calls Bezetha there has been found a site, dated 150 BC – 70 AD which contained a number of grottoes with steps leading down to them. There are also rectangular stone basins. Nearby is a spring which works like a self-flushing lavatory system and this could explain the movement described by John. There are relics of votive offerings dedicated to Asclepius and Serapis – pagan gods of healing. This healing sanctuary could therefore be very old, going back to Canaanite days. Such places often transcend religious boundaries and are used in defiance of ancient codes.

All this underlines the importance, both of archaeology and geography of the Holy Land. It is only in recent years that this part of the world has been open widely to the public at large. Some Bible scholars have never visited Israel, Bultmann for example, and they are at a disadvantage. John Robinson made a close study of the topography and drew out some useful lessons. He was convinced that John wrote his Gospel while Jerusalem was still standing.

7. *While I am moving, someone else is in the pool before me.* The description of the healing place given above shows what happens. The steps down to the basins were very narrow and could not accommodate more than one patient with his bearers.

9. *It was the Sabbath.* The incident turns into a conflict about sabbath keeping and we are back in the atmosphere of the Synoptics where there was conflict between Jesus and the Pharisees about the same subject.

17. *My Father keeps on working and so do I.* There was a Greek thought that God is ceaselessly active and some Jewish rabbis taught that God could do as he likes in the world without breaking the Sabbath because 1) the whole world was no more than his private residence – Isaiah 6:3) he fills the whole world – Jeremiah 23:24.

John uses the charge about sabbath breaking and the claim of equality with God to introduce a block of teaching about 1) the authority of Jesus vv 19-30. Note here the parallel teaching in the Synoptics – Matthew 10: 32,33, Luke 12:8.9,10:22.

2) the theme of witness both by the works of Jesus and by scriptures vv30 – 40.

3) condemnation of the Jews who do not believe the witness.

John is aware that the whole mission of Jesus is under attack by the Jewish leaders and counters this with clear teaching about the relationship of the Son to the Father. So the discourse ends because the healing of the ruler's son and the crippled man has now been provided with its proper theological meaning (Hoskyns).

CHAPTER SIX

A KING'S FEAST

This chapter is concerned with the feeding of the multitude and the aftermath. We may know this sign or miracle very well because it is recorded by all the evangelists but have not read on to understand the upheaval which, according to John, was caused. He shows it was a time of decision for many of the crowd who were fed. They wanted to make him a king and had Jesus allowed it, his ministry would have turned into the direct confrontation which took place a year later when a demonstration accompanied his entry into Jerusalem and he was arrested soon afterwards.

The fact that all the Gospels describe this wonderful feeding must make us take it very seriously. Why was it seen as a significant incident in Our Lord's ministry? I suggest the reason was that it fulfilled part of the Jewish expectation about the kingdom of God. The Jews were waiting for God to bring in his kingdom by destroying their nation's enemies, by inviting his people to a banquet and by introducing a new age of peace and prosperity into this world. St. Mark shows clearly that the enemies Jesus destroyed were sin, ignorance, sickness and death but all evangelists record the miraculous feeding which could symbolise the divine feast. The new age following the resurrection was yet to come. So the signs pointed increasingly to Jesus as the leader who would bring in God's kingdom.

1. The chapter starts with a connecting phrase which could be translated 'after that' but more accurately "after some time". Chapter Five had ended with Jesus in Jerusalem but we now find him in Galilee. This is the longest stay in Galilee recorded in John. Jesus seems to have spent the winter there and indeed we do not find him in Jerusalem again until the following autumn. This seems to deny that the writer John is a Jerusalem rather than a Galilee disciple, as has been suggested. *Across the Sea of Galilee.* There has been some speculation about where this incident took place. It would seem that it was in the area of Decapolis in a direct line with Magdala, a town which has since disappeared but was south of Capernaum. Robinson suggests a place, Kursi (Gerasa?) or Hippos which is the modern En Gev, well-known to today's pilgrim because steamer trips go there from Capernaum and fish and chip lunches can be bought. The sea there is full of Peter fish and these are caught and cooked fresh. Behind the modern kibbutz the ground rises to low hills where the miracle could have taken place.

4. *The Passover, a feast of the Jews.* So it was spring and the grass would be green. Generally commentators pass this statement as fair comment but it does prompt the question why John needed to add "a feast of the Jews". Jews at home and abroad would not need to be told this because it was the main feast of the Jewish year. In fact we have seen that the Gospel might have been written in the end for expatriate Jews. These may in time have collected Gentile friends who were interested in hearing this unique narrative. Or an editor might have added it later. We can see the hand of such an editor in several places in this Gospel.

9. *Two fish.* The Greek word means "cooked fish – or pickled? We know there was a pickling factory at Galilee.

11. Jesus took the food, gave thanks (eucharisto) and gave to the crowd. This would be the procedure for any head of a family before a meal. There is no need to suppose that John was influenced by the Synoptists' account of the Last Supper but he might have had in mind what the Church was continuing to do after the Resurrection.

14. *Surely this is that prophet.* Here we have proof of the very sensitive times in which Jesus carried out his ministry. The air was full of expectation for one who would rescue Israel from the Roman occupier. Jesus defused the situation by withdrawing into the hills. He would be anxious that his disciples should not be caught up in the demonstration. In fact, they also slipped away and returned across the lake toward Capernaum.

19. *Walking on the sea.* It should be said here that the Greek could be translated "beside the sea". The suggestion has been made that the disciples saw him and realised in panic that they were too close to the shore. However, Jesus came to them and was taken aboard.

22. *Next morning the crowd was standing on the opposite shore.* No doubt they hoped Jesus would reappear, knowing that he had not left with his disciples. As we have seen Jesus joined them in the boat. Was it perhaps an agreed plan? Anyway Jesus arrived in Capernaum before the crowd.

26. This starts a teaching session on the need for understanding the significance of the feeding of the crowd. The Jews have only a short-sighted view both of this "sign" and indeed of the whole saving work of God. They looked for a divine kingdom to be set up in this world rather than for one out of it. Their minds turn no doubt to the way God fed his people in the wilderness with manna when they were on their way to the promised land. So the feeding by Jesus of the multitude is seen as a sign that he will lead them to victory in this world. They cannot penetrate through the work of Jesus to the spiritual dimension. This is the story of the whole Gospel until the Resurrection opens the eyes of his closest disciples to the true nature of his mission.

35. *Sir, give us this bread now and always.* The Jews misunderstood what Jesus said just as the Samaritan woman at the well failed to understand Jesus' reference to living water (4:15). They cannot see the spiritual connotation.

35. *I am the bread of life.* This is probably better translated "the bread which gives life". This is altogether too much for his audience who thinks he is trespassing on God's preserve. This is the first of the claims by Jesus. He is the bread of life, the light of the world, the door of the sheep, the good shepherd, the vine, the resurrection and the way. We today can work out these metaphors but what would the Jews of that day understand by these expressions? They might get some help from Old Testament symbols but this would assume some theological learning. So Jesus is no longer speaking to the Galilean crowd but to learned men. In fact we are told the "Jews" take part in the discussion and by this name John normally means the Jewish authorities in Jerusalem. No doubt some had travelled north to find out what was going on.

What would they have understood by "the bread of life"? Barrett notes that "it is of primary importance that the manna was interpreted in the wisdom tradition of Israel in terms of word and instruction" God feeds men by his word. Jesus is his word.[22]

But Jesus takes the theme further and talks about the bread being his flesh. For John this is an extension of the phrase in the Prologue – "the word was made flesh". This is too much for the Jews. They have already protested against the saying, "I am the bread which came down from heaven". The idea of eating Jesus to gain eternal life worries them still more.

54. *Whoever eats my flesh and drinks my blood possesses eternal life.* There is little dispute that these words refer to the Eucharist. We need to remember that John was writing after the Resurrection when the Eucharist was established as part of the daily routine of the first Christians (Acts 2:42) St. Luke's statement that "he was known to them in the breaking of bread" at Emmaus (24:35)) would have become the experience of all disciples in the post-Resurrection Christian community. They were living in an atmosphere of Easter every day. To them the Lord was not merely in the past nor yet in the future but very much a present companion, alive in their midst, giving joy and strength to those who had been baptised into his family. This is the kind of experience which the Church needs to recapture today and some steps were taken at Vatican 11 toward it but we still have a long way to go.

59. *Many of his disciples on hearing it exclaimed, 'this is more than we can stomach'.* The resurrection had still to happen and we find that at Capernaum there was a strong reaction against his teaching by some of the outer ring of disciples. At this point we might consider the effect which this debate was having on the ordinary citizen who would be looking on without understanding the phrases which were being tossed about. They had seen the miracle or sign and were

convinced that Jesus had some special relationship with God. Some saw and simply believed. But it was clear that others were seeing without belief. In the end only further understanding could come after the Lord's resurrection when the words 'bread of life' could be comprehended without Old Testament imagery.

Jesus challenged the twelve disciples about leaving him but they have seen enough to know that he was the only one to reveal the things of God.

71. *Yet one of you is a devil.* If we think this is a drastic remark we might remember that a similar accusation had been levelled at Peter (Mark 8:33).

William Temple notes that Judas probably shared the excitement that followed the miracle of feeding. A great opportunity was offered and the Master threw it away.

But whereas some disciples just went away, it was Judas' great sin that he remained and became the Achilles heel of the Lord's ministry.

Some commentators hint that John may be putting the record straight here about Mark's statement that Jesus called Peter Satan (8:33). Simon Peter and Simon Iscariot (father of Judas) have Simon in common. But this is perhaps stretching the text too far. When somebody does wrong Satan has taken him over as an ally.

We can learn from this chapter about the importance of the Eucharist from the earliest days. Looking back from this side of the resurrection we understand the full significance of the words of Jesus, "I am the bread of life".

We can also echo Peter's words, "Lord to whom shall we go? You have the words of eternal life". There is no other salvation except through the revelation of Jesus Christ.

CHAPTER SEVEN

A JEWISH FEAST

In this chapter we find the last public debate with the Jewish authorities in Jerusalem but we first have to get Jesus from Galilee where he appears to have been for a year. At first sight it seems as if Jesus is being less than straightforward. He tells his brethren that he is not going up to the Feast of Tabernacles or Tents but then goes up later. However if we take John's chronology as the correct one we know that Jesus was in great danger in Jerusalem. He therefore knew that to be swept into the festival by Galilaeans

33

who had tried to make him king would be asking for trouble – and his hour had not yet come. So he slips quietly into Jerusalem after the feast had started. John paints a picture of restless excitement there. Everybody is looking for Jesus, hoping no doubt that he will decide to use this popular festival for bringing in his kingdom.

3. *His brothers.* There has been some speculation about whether they were actual brothers. The Greek *adelphoi* can mean kinsmen. Here they are contrasted with the disciples. There is a suggestion that Jesus has his own disciples in Jerusalem. So there is an attempt in Galilee to persuade Jesus to go down to the city and test opinion there. This would be in the style of other rebel leaders who forced a confrontation and were defeated. It was never to be Jesus' way.

10. *When his brothers had gone down to the festival.* Are the disciples included in this? We are told that Jesus finally went down alone and yet in 9:2 we find disciples involved with a man born blind from birth. If John lived in the city to carry out work as Zebedee's agent, there could have been a group of disciples round him.

Certainly a crowd of Galilaeans went down for the feast and one scholar has suggested this politically motivated mob was the cause of the blood bath mentioned in Luke 13: 1 – 3. This might have caused a rift between Herod and Pilate which was only healed the following year (Luke 23:12).

All this is speculation but it would tie up some loose ends in the four Gospels and would account for the renewed hostility against Jesus when he comes to Jerusalem.

I am indebted to John Robinson (Priority of John pp 21 seq.) for showing that John was very precise about time and place in chapters 7 – 10. If we accept that the cleansing of the Temple (chapter 2) took place in 27 AD we can see that we are here in the period late 28 – to early 29. It is also possible with patience to work out when the different Jewish feasts occurred at that time. In this John differs from the Synoptics.

In 29 AD the Feast of Tabernacles happened on October 12th. It started with the illumination of the Temple with the light of lamps and candles and there was ceremonial dancing (Dictionary of the Bible-Mackenzie). On the last day there was ritual pouring out of water, a libation which was meant to encourage rains necessary for good crops. In the middle east there is great concern about rainfall. During a recent visit to Cyprus (only a short distance from Israel) I found the people almost willing it to rain heavily.

It is possible to produce a diary of events for this part of Jesus' ministry:

October 12th	Festival begins
15th	Jesus arrives halfway through the feast. Teaches in the Temple (7:14) Teaches in the Treasury (8:20)
18/19th	Pouring of the water libation. Jesus makes claim about streams of flowing water Jesus teaches in the Treasury where the light of great golden candlestick was lit during the feast. "I am the light of the world". Jesus goes to the Pool of Siloam which was not far from the Temple. He cures a blind man with subsequent argument.
December 20 – 27	Feast of Dedication (winter). Also called the Feast of Lights and celebrated the recovery and rededication of the Temple by Judas Maccabaeus in 165 BC. There was an exchange of gifts, Christmas style.

January 30 AD. We find Jesus in Bethany beyond Jordan and he is there long enough for an audience to be built up (10:40). He is recalled reluctantly to raise Lazarus from the dead. This raising of Lazarus redoubles the efforts of Jewish authorities to arrest Jesus and he retreats to Ephraim.

Such dating of events leading up to the arrest and prosecution of Jesus does not indicate the mere meditations of an old man at the end of the first century but rather the narrative of someone still close to the actual events.

We are now ready to return to the text of Chapter 7.

10. *He went up himself.* Our Lord's timing was perfect. It he had gone up before the festival began, it might not have started because of a riot and he would have been blamed. The symbolism of water and light, too, was important for his teaching. Jesus did not have to take the initiative because people were awaiting to hear from him, and this is always an advantage for a teacher.

12. John paints well the picture of a Jerusalem agog with interest about Jesus. Rumour was rife and one is reminded of its description by Virgil in Aeneid Book 4, "Rumour of all evils the most swift. Speed lends her strength and she wins vigour as she goes – virisque adquirit eundo". We learn what an impression Jesus had built up during his former visits to the city. Interest could have heightened if there had been some slaughter of Galilaeans.

14. *Began to teach.* For the next three chapters we have Jesus caught up in sharp controversy. Through his relationship with God he has to speak in a dimension

which the Jews cannot understand. Central to the Jews' questioning seems to be the problem, How can this man be a saviour? The nation's expectation was something quite different from the way Jesus was acting. They expected God to intervene with power irresistibly but here was somebody speaking on equal terms with them. Their perplexity could be illustrated today by the unease caused when a Russian leader suddenly starts walkabouts.

In the end, Jesus has to appeal to them at the lowest level – if you do not understand at least judge from the works I am doing. Perhaps here we see the true importance of his miracles. They were evidence at its most basic for a divine phenomenon or happening.

14 – 24. Attempt to come to terms with an untrained man speaking with authority about God and interpreting the Law.

25 – 36. Could Jesus be the Messiah in view of his well-known human origin? Jesus asserts he comes from God. There is an attempt to arrest him. Jesus says he comes from God and is going to God.

37 – 44. Jesus takes advantage of the Tabernacles' ritual of pouring out water to teach that the Spirit would be poured out as never before.

45 – 52. The Jewish authorities reproach the police who had bungled the arrest of Jesus. Nicodemus intervenes.

The debate continues in the next chapter but we might take note of the following points. This encounter between Jesus and the Jews has a parallel in Luke 4: 16 – 30.

The Jews of the Dispersion (35) meant the expatriate Jews who since the Exile in Babylon (c.700 BC) had chosen to remain abroad and earn a living in other Mediterranean and Middle East countries.

The reference to Galilee reminds us of the North/South divide of the Holy Land. After Solomon's successful reign (c.900 BC) the North had seceded from the South, appointed its own king and made provision for parallel worship.

This rift had been mostly healed with the return from exile (c.500 BC) except for the region of Samaria where half caste Jews lived and continued their own worship on Mount Gerizim. However, the suspicion remained that Galilee preferred to be independent and go its own way apart from Jerusalem. It was very close to Gentile country anyway.

The outpouring of water. The words of the prophet Zechariah were much in mind, "On that day living water shall issue from Jerusalem, half flowing to the eastern sea and half to the western, in summer and winter alike. Then the Lord shall become king over all the earth." (14:8).

Today we may learn from this attempt to come to terms with the person of Jesus. It is all too easy to dismiss him as a holy man whom the later Christian Church elevated to the position of the Son of God. John reports clearly the claim of Jesus to come from God and to return to him. Only when he is seen with this background can his teaching assume an unique authority. So it must be obeyed by his followers on pain of eternal death.

CHAPTER EIGHT

THE FATHER'S SON

This chapter begins with the story of the woman taken in adultery. It is not found in every version because there is doubt whether it was in the original Gospel. Some texts do not have it. It is more in the style of the Synoptics but there are no grounds for supposing it to be unhistorical. It is an incident not out of keeping with the approach of Jesus to similar challenges. He is the champion of those who have been mauled by the Law.

12. *I am the Light of the world.* The Feast of Tabernacles was also called the festival of Light just as Hindus have their Diwali where there are great illuminations. Our Lord's words, therefore are very apt.

The idea of God being like a light is a familiar one in the Bible. Jesus is like a light because he shows us the way to God – our path is illuminated. "Your word is a lamp for my feet" (Ps. 119:105).

13. *Your testimony is not valid.* So the fierce debate between Jesus and the Jews is renewed. Once again we should remind ourselves that this is taking place in a narrow Jewish setting. For centuries religion had been in the hands of professional exponents of the Law. For the most part any personal devotional life based on a loving relationship with Godhad been squeezed out by an intricate manipulation of the Law which left ordinary people abandoned. It was in protest against this dry religion that Qumran had been founded with its emphasis on complete sanctification of life. It is true that the keeping of the Law was also the aim of this community but, as we have seen earlier there was an idea of atonement involved – a few making sacrifices for the many. The inspiration of all religious parties, however, was a materialistic kingdom of God in the future. This kingdom would be brought about here, in this world by a recognisable Messiah sent by God. The Jewish religion still is very much based in this world. This is shown in a recent book, The Resurrection of Jesus, by a Rabbi, Pinchas Lapide. He accepts the resurrection of Jesus but not his Messiahship because a new Jerusalem of peace and prosperity on earth did not follow the event. Jesus' talk of belonging to another world above (8:23) and of a relationship there with the Father would have sounded strangely in Jewish ears.

In the distant past Abraham and Moses had walked with God and had a special relationship with him but nothing like that had happened since the prophets and they had died out 500 years before.

It should also be remembered that Jesus was speaking in a far smaller Jerusalem than today. The Temple would have overshadowed daily life and within its porticos new rabbis were being trained in the all important Law – St. Paul might have been one of them. Such young fanatics would have deeply resented Jesus' style of teaching, even if some older rabbis took a more philosophical attitude. So it will be seen that the background against which Jesus was teaching was not helpful to new concepts about the Father and his love.

17. *The testimony of two witnesses is valid.* However Jesus sometimes uses a Jewish argument. Having proper witnesses was very important in Jewish law.

22. *Will he kill himself?* The idea of Jesus escaping permanently could only be explained by 1) suicide 2) going to the dispersion. Here is another example of the failure to understand the dimension in which Jesus spoke.

28. *When you have lifted up the Son of Man.* This is one of the ways in which Jesus teaches his coming death. See also 3:14 and 12:32. By the time we come to the actual Passion Jesus has so prepared his followers for its significance that the events of his arrest, trial and crucifixion have merely to be recorded without comment.

29. *I have been taught by my father.* In John's gospel the answer to Jesus' closeness to the Father is not that he is God but he is the son. Jesus is as close to God as a son is to a father. Elsewhere (10:34) Jesus is to justify this sonship by quoting one of the Psalms.

Here we should give further thought to this recurring theme in John, the relationship of Jesus to God the Father. Later Christian thought came to terms with it but we might ask what this could mean to Jews whose central and unmoveable belief was, Hear, O Israel, the Lord our God is one God. Greek religion might allow a more human conception of the divine but Jewish monotheism was absolute.

I am indebted to A.E. Harvey's book, Jesus and the Constraints of History, for helpful guidance. In the seventh chapter he discusses how this idea of the son of God could be contained within such monotheism.[23] He shows how the Jewish idea of a father/son relationship which is completely different from ours, throws light on the language of Jesus. Three points are important. 1) The son had to give obedience above all to his father. It was part of the Law and disobedience was punishable by death. In the ancient world this kind of filial obedience was paralleled by the service a subject owed a king or a slave his master. In the Bible men were called sons of God when they gave him perfect obedience. Therefore to say that Jesus was a son of God meant first of all that he obeyed the divine will perfectly. See Hebrews 5: 8 – 9.

2) a son was expected to learn from his father as an apprentice might sit at the feet of a master. Thus a teacher could be called a father to his pupils. A father passed down his wisdom, knowledge and experience to his son. This is echoed in our Lord's words in 5: 19 – 20. The son does nothing on his own unless he sees his father doing it. The Jews longed for someone to show them God's nature and commands. To some it seemed that Jesus was this revealer and so he could again be called a son of God.

3) The Jews have always been strong in commerce and trade and in this it was important that a man had a good agent if he wanted to expand his business. Who could be a more reliable agent than one's own son? The fact that a son had both to obey his father and to learn from him gave him the necessary qualities of agent. An agent's position was very strong – he stood in the place of his master and had to be obeyed as such. Jesus spoke of himself as being sent by the Father and this would have meant to a Jew that he claimed to be God's agent. This theme of Jesus as the authorised agent of God runs throughout John's Gospel but we can see it used in the Synoptics. This is not to say that the Jews accepted Jesus as the son of God. It was his charge that they did not, even though he showed them excellent credentials but they could have understood what he was saying. Later generations of Christians looking at the Gospel from this side of the resurrection were able to complete the picture.

33. *We are Abraham's descendants ... we have never been in slavery.* The Jews were proud of their founding father, Abraham, who left the security of the city of Ur in modern Iraq and went out into the unknown with his tribe and brought a new people into existence. It was untrue to say they had never been in bondage politically but here they are claiming to be the free children of God. No matter how much they suffered at the hands of other nations, they preserved a spiritual superiority. This led to the idea that they were well and had no need of a physician – an attitude which Jesus condemned. Jesus says here that anybody who commits sin is a slave and therefore has forfeited the right to be a member of God's family. Only penitence can enable them to be brought back.

35. *The slave has no permanent standing.* Jesus reminds them of a fact they would know that a slave has no rights. This is contrasted with the status of a son who had a right to everything in his father's house. It is this privilege Jesus is offering through his teaching.

39. *If you were Abraham's children.* Abraham obeyed God's call. Now Jesus is repeating that call to truth but the Jews do not obey. They are not acting like Abraham. Handsome is as handsome does!

41. *We are not base-born (born of fornication).* This could well be a sneer at Jesus' birth. There might have been a rumour that there was something irregular about his birth. It could also refer to a debased Jewish religion such as the Samaritan sect into which foreign elements had been imported centuries before.

44. *Your father is a devil.* This is a difficult passage. There is a contrast here with the God who created everything good at the beginning and the devil who damaged that good creation. Jesus is trying to recreate his Father's good world but the Jews are opposing his work. Therefore they are of the devil.

48. *You are a Samaritan.* As we have seen Samaritans were a despised sect so to call a person one was an insult.

53. *Are you greater than our Father Abraham?* There is a comparison here between the great figures of the Old Testament and Jesus the incarnate son of God. Lightfoot says, "whereas Abraham (like the Baptist 1:6.) came into existence at a definite moment, the word of God is above and beyond time". So it would be correct for Jesus to say, Before Abraham was, I am".[24]

The Jews regarded this claim as blasphemous and prepare to hand out the punishment for blasphemy within Jewish Law – stoning.

CHAPTER NINE

THE MAN BORN BLIND

The last chapter was full of bitter debate and Jesus was obviously in danger of being arrested at any time. That he was not was probably due to the fact that people were divided in Jerusalem about whether he was a good man or bad (7:35). This next chapter is a more straightforward narrative of a healing miracle and resembles similar miracles in the Synoptics. Prophets in the Old Testament had foretold that the Messiah would open the eyes of the blind (Isaiah 29:18).

2. *Rabbi who sinned...?* This is a question still asked today when some kind of illness or disaster happens. The idea that God punishes us in this world because a family sins is familiar. This cannot be so and is rejected even in the Old Testament (Ezekiel 18:2). Here the prophet quotes the parable, "the fathers have eaten sour grapes and the children's teeth are set on edge" and says this is not so. The man who sins shall die for his own sins. In fact in the Gospels the idea that sin is linked to illness is found. The forgiveness of sin by Jesus is followed by a cure (Mark 2:8).

3. *So that God's power might be displayed.* We have to be careful here that we do not think that the man was made blind so that Jesus could show his healing power – a passive subject for Jesus' ministry. Although the Greek gives this sense we should understand 'so that' as a consecutive clause. The man was born blind and so became a candidate for the healing work of the Messiah. Lightfoot suggests that we may compare St. Paul's ready acceptance of his weaknesses as giving opportunity for the revelation of divine strength (2 Corinthians 12:9.10).[25]

4. *While daylight lasts.* The life of Jesus is compared to a day's work ending with the dark. Night time without modern means of illumination has always effectively cut down human activity and so every moment of daytime has to be used. The monastic rule of St. Benedict was very much geared to the best use of daylight hours.

5. *I am the light.* Before the miracle takes place, its significance is pointed out.

6. *He spat.* In the ancient world spittle was believed to have medicinal value cp. Mark 8:23.

7. *Pool of Siloam.* This can still be seen in Jerusalem. Water for the libations at the feast of Tabernacles was drawn from here and was a forecast of the blessings of the coming Messianic age. The name 'the sent one' is used by John for Jesus. The early Church which used anointing at Baptism saw the symbolic significance of this incident.

8. *His neighbours.* The consequence of this miracle are now convincingly set out by John. We would expect the man's friends to be mystified by what had happened. We would expect the Jewish authorities to make some investigation especially since the miracle took place on the sabbath.

We are given an interesting picture of how the Jewish council exercised the small amount of power still left to it. It is reminiscent of the inquisitorial courts of the later Christian Church in decadent times.

14. *The Sabbath day.* Since Jesus seems to be on the run from this authority he would not be able to choose his day for curing people. He had already posed the question "Is it permitted to do good or to do evil on the Sabbath, to save life or to kill?" (Mark 3:4) and there was no doubt what was his own verdict.

Two further points need to be considered in this chapter because they touch on the date and authority of the writer.

18. *The Jews would not believe.* Barrett says that John speaks indiscriminately of 'the Jews' and 'the Pharisees' because he has no clear knowledge of conditions in Palestine before 70 AD but Robinson disputes this and says that John more

than the other writers is aware of the differences and divisions in pre-70 AD Palestine. The word 'Jews' or Judaioi in Greek may stand for those in authority or those who live in the southern part of Palestine, or sometimes as a contrast with Galilaeans, Gentiles or non-Palestinians. Robinson writes, "Often, of course 'the Jews' are generally the 'authorities' but when they alternate with the 'Pharisees' it may be possible to detect a distinction of roles. Thus, in the healing of the blind man in Ch. 9 it is the Pharisees who object to the healing on religious grounds because it breaks the sabbath law. But in verses 18 – 34 it is the Jews who interrogate him (just as they do the cripple in 5:10–15). They represent the hierarchy and their interest is whether he has really been cured. Is it a certifiable cure? For, ascertaining this is their job (cf Mark 1.44, Show yourself to the priest ... that will certify the cure). But even when the medical facts are apparently beyond dispute they try to make him disavow the ground of healing; and when he will not, they lay him under the ban which they alone have the power to serve".[26]

So they cast him out – of the synagogue.

22. *The Jews agreed to expel from the synagogue*... There is a technical Greek word here, aposynagogus. Some scholars say this word was only applicable after the final split between Jews and Christians late in the first century but evidence of this kind of action is not clear and only competence to lead a service was involved. There are several references to harrassment of Christians in the New Testament of a similar nature but all these events took place in the 30s, 40s and early 50s and none of the predictions in the main body of John's Gospel need reflect anything later than that.

So from all this, it would seem that a late date for John is by no means proved – rather the opposite.

CHAPTER TEN

THE GOOD SHEPHERD

The image of Jesus, the Good Shepherd, has been very popular with the Church through the ages but in recent times has been over-sentimentalised. But, as we shall see, there are strong lessons to be learnt from this title.

The theme of sheep and shepherd is a powerful one in the Old Testament as we would expect within a people much engaged in farming. Even in Israel today sheep and goats with their shepherds are to be seen everywhere. These men are often fierce individuals who resent any intrusion upon their flocks. A tourist trying to take a photo can be roughly repulsed. They will also lead their sheep and goats fearlessly across main roads in the face of fast-moving traffic. They go ahead to clear a way.

Chapter 34 of Ezekiel should be read to see something of the background of St. John's words on shepherds.

1 – 3. I am grateful to John Robinson for suggesting in an essay that there are two parables in these verses. Here we have two candidates presenting themselves for admission by the doorkeeper to the sheepfold. One is a thief and robber, the other is the true shepherd and this must be Jesus himself. But who is the doorkeeper? It could be the religious authorities of the Jews who are meant to be like watchmen on the walls and protect the sheep inside. Would they be able to recognise Jesus the true shepherd, who comes from God and has a right to enter? The signs are that they would not but would allow the wrong men to enter. The Jews cannot recognise the real shepherd. Why? because they are blind. Here is a reference to the last chapter.

There is a link here with the warnings of Jesus in the Synoptics about thieves who threaten property (Luke 12:33.39. Matthew 6:19 fol). Such warnings might apply to the Second Coming but it is more likely that they refer to the reception of Jesus as he comes to Jerusalem, seeking to be accepted. But the Jewish leaders prefer thieves and robbers. It is interesting that the word for robber or bandit was used for Barabbas who was preferred to Jesus (18:40).

Jesus in every age has to be accepted as the true shepherd who comes seeking his sheep. We might note Revelation 3:20 where Jesus stands at the door and knocks. Note also James 5:9 where the judge stands "before the doors".

4. *When he has brought them all out.* The parable now changes and we have the theme of the relationship of a shepherd to his sheep. Apparently different flocks can be shut up in the same sheepfold but the true shepherd's sheep recognise his voice. A good shepherd goes in front of his flock to head off any dangers. We have noted above that this still happens.

14. *I am the door of the sheepfold.* Again, the metaphor changes and the relationship of shepherd and sheep is explored to the utmost. Just as there is only one entrance to a sheep pen so there is only one way to the Father and this is through the Son. This is a tremendous saying which should be remembered when multi-faith religion is mentioned. This was the faith of the first Christians as shown in Acts 4:12, "There is no salvation in anyone else at all..."

10.*I have come that men may have life.* Hoskyns notes, "the evangelist now reaches the supreme christian truth ... The theme is life and life through the voluntary death of Jesus. It is his willingness to die that marks him as the good shepherd".

43

14. *I am the good shepherd.* The Greek word used here for "good" is not what we might expect, "agathos (morally good)", but "kalos" which means 'attractive', 'of fine appearance'. In his "Readings in St. John Gospel" 'William Temple makes an important point. He writes, "it is important that the word for 'good' here is one which represents not moral rectitude of goodness, nor its austerity but its attractiveness. We must not forget that our vocation is so to practise virtue that men are won to it : it is possible to be morally upright repulsively! In the Lord we see the beauty of holiness".[27]

If we wish to gain others for Christ we must make our life attractive and this is shown in our readiness to make sacrifices for others as Jesus laid down his life for the sheep.

15. *I lay down my life for the sheep.* Here again Jesus gives a reason for his coming death on the Cross.

17. *The Father loves me.* Here Jesus refers again to his special relationship with his Father which is a bone of contention with the Jews who are split on their verdict on Jesus.

22. Feast of Dedication. This celebrated the recovery of the Temple from heathen hands in 165 BC. It was held in December and so it would be cold in Jerusalem. It would be warmer in the portico of the Temple and Jesus is found there. Once again curiosity about the mission of Jesus boils up. Jews gather round him to discover if he is the expected messiah. Again, great difficulty arises about different concepts of messiahship. Jesus is the promised one but not the expected all-conquering military leader. So he asks them to make a judgment about the miracles he does. If they are not from God, how are they done?

25. *My deeds done in my Father's name.* Here again Jesus teaches about his close relationship with the Father and ends with the outstanding statement, "I and my Father are one". This shocks the Jews who once again try to kill him by stoning. We may well ask how far Jesus goes in spelling out a theology of his relationship with the Father. In fact it was left to a much later generation of Christian scholars to get to grips with Christology and a doctrine of the Trinity. If we place this Gospel at the end of the first century as some scholars do, we might expect the beginning of a theology of the person of Christ. But if John is writing soon after the events we would not expect such philosophising and, in fact, we find the writer not a bit interested in the how of the Incarnation. He is content to describe the earthly life of Jesus. As was indicated in the notes on Chapter 8, the relationship between father and son in Middle Eastern life could be transferred to that of Jesus with God his father. A good son would reflect his father's image. To be a son is to show the character, to reproduce the thought and action of another, whether it be Abraham, the Devil or God. To claim to be a son of God is not blasphemy as the Jews

protested. They should have known their Bible better. So Jesus can be seen to be on the same metaphysical level as every other son of God, yet in action he is unique because he "alone does what is acceptable to him". Robinson thinks this argument could not have been invented later but carries us back to the very early Christian teaching. John sees Jesus as unique and indicates this by reserving the name "son" for Jesus as against "children of God" for Christians.

Jesus can say "I and the Father are one' (10:30), 'the Father is in me and I in the Father' (38) because he is acting as his father would (37) and 'his deeds are done in God's name.' (25)

14. *Other sheep.* This could be the non-believing Jews, the Greek speaking Jews or the Gentiles who have yet to be brought in. Barrett notes that this remark is recorded in the context of a Gentile mission.

18. *I am laying it down of my own free will.* The early Church was very anxious to show that Jesus accepted death voluntarily. Here John is again preparing us for the reason for the crucifixion. In v.15 Jesus says he is laying down his life for the sheep.

40. *Jesus withdrew again.* To Bethany beyond Jordan where we found John baptising in Chapter One.

CHAPTER ELEVEN

LAZARUS

The problem with this part of the Gospel lies not so much with the actual text which is straightforward but whether the incident should be there at all. Some scholars think this was not part of the original Fourth Gospel. The Roman Catholic scholar, R.E. Brown thinks it would be easier to reconcile the sequence of events in John with the Synoptics if chapters 11 – 12 were removed. But if we assume that John is writing independently of the other three evangelists we do not have this problem. In fact, it would not be easy to fit the Lazarus incident into the Synoptics' pattern for they give us only one visit by Jesus to the South. Since the Lazarus narrative implies a continuing acquaintance of Jesus with Jerusalem society, there would be no place for it in the plan of the other writers who mention only one visit to Jerusalem and that immediately before the Passion. They clearly see the entrance into Jerusalem and the cleansing of the Temple as the cause for the arrest and trial of our Lord. In John this cleansing takes place at the beginning of his ministry and although this caused considerable alarm, it was not the final provocation. Rather is it the raising of Lazarus which fanned the flames of popular admiration for Jesus and sent the authorities away to make the arrangements for his arrest.

We find further mention of this Lazarus incident in 11:45 and 12:1,9,1,9,17. Also although we should not be too influenced by apocryphal writings, it is worth mentioning that the Secret Gospel of Mark gives an account of the raising of Lazarus.

Hoskyn's judgment is worth considering; "the story as it stands is Johannine throughout. It is not only in itself a complete literary unity but is so closely interwoven into the texture of the whole gospel as to be unintelligible apart from its relation to the whole gospel. Wherever it is possible to check the author's literary method, it is clear that he is working on traditional material that in part at least can be identified in the Synoptic Gospels"[28] – St. Luke for example, 10:38. Hoskyns adds that he does not think that John created the story to underline any teaching about Jesus.

3. *The sisters sent a message to him.* Jesus is still in retirement in the other Bethany – beyond Jordan. He knows that any return to Jerusalem could bring the last chapter of his ministry. He had escaped only with difficulty death by stoning 10:31.

6. *Jesus waited for two days.* This was not to intensify the coming miracle but to consider whether he should go at all. The making of such a decision has been called another Gethsemane. Is it the father's will that he should go to certain death? No doubt this was a time of agonising prayer. The disciples know the situation and warn him v.7 that only a short time ago there had been an attempt upon his life. Thomas calls for courage v.16 to accompany the Master on this dangerous journey.

19. *Many people.* This Bethany unlike the other was a short distance from the city so people could easily walk there and full publicity would be given to his return from the edge of the country.

Jesus arrives at the house of mourning. He asks to see the burial place and a conversation takes place about resurrection. Jesus promises that Lazarus will come back to life but Mary can only think of the last resurrection.

24. *I know he will rise again at the resurrection on the last day.* This was the standard belief of the Pharisees. The Sadducees did not believe in a future life.

25. *I am the resurrection and the life.* Lightfoot notes that Martha has asked for a gift from God v.22.[29] Jesus replies that the gift is a personal communication of the Lord himself who has taken human nature upon him precisely in order to impart this gift. For those who believe in him, death has lost its sting – so far from having power to destroy, it is the gate of life. Hoskyns notes that what is to the Jews a future hope, is to Christians a present reality. This is spelt out more simply in 1 John 5:12. "He who has the Son has life ..." Resurrection and life are found only in Jesus, as Barrett notes.[30] All this has been taught by Jesus.

Anybody who takes up his cross and follows Jesus will have eternal life.

But Martha cannot go this far. She can only believe Jesus is the Messiah who has come into the world. This was the imperfect confession of the multitude in 6:14.

He sighed and was deeply moved. The Greek word used here is "to be painfully moved, indignant". Was Jesus distressed because he saw the trouble and sorrow which death brought to people, the extent of the Devil's grip on mankind? He goes on "to weep".

41. *Father, I thank thee; thou has heard me.* Here we have a clear example that Jesus does not claim to do miracles on his own like a Greek divine man. Robinson notes, "the miracles are entirely and solely the works of the Father", – see also 5:33.36., 9:3 fol. The son only has power because it is given him by the Father. We might like to compare Matthew 26:53 where Jesus says in Gethsemane, "do you suppose that I cannot speak to my father who would at once send to my aid more than twelve legions of angels?" There is no suggestion here that he could defeat them because he was God. So we have the same picture in John. All his power comes from a prayerful dependence on the Father. He can act because he is heard.

So outside the tomb of Lazarus onlookers might learn of the dependence of Jesus on his Father. Lazarus is brought back to life and Jesus gains more followers but others return to the city and report the facts to the Pharisees. They now take the action which will lead to his arrest and trial.

47. *The Chief Priests and Pharisees convene a meeting.* There has been a difficulty of fitting in the two trials of Jesus into the last twelve hours of his earthly life. The illegality of the night trial by the Jewish authorities in the early hours of Maundy Thursday has always been a problem. But if we suppose this trial had been held some weeks before in Jesus' absence this difficulty is removed. This would have been in accordance with the known Roman practice where a proscription or prographe made it possible for authorities in the absence of the offender to pronounce him guilty until proved otherwise and therefore liable to arrest on sight. We find examples of this in Roman writings where a price is put on the head of one found guilty. A search is started and good rewards (thirty pieces of silver?) were paid for information leading to arrest and execution. When the criminal was found he was not tried again but the judgement was carried out unless there was good reason for not doing so. Although there were some legal procedures to be followed, no doubt in the case of proscribed persons incrimination would precede interrogation and this happened in the case of Jesus when he was finally brought before important men on the Council.

If this line is followed we can make more sense of the trials of Jesus after his arrest in Gethsemane. More comment will be made when we reach the Passion narrative. However, it is worth noting that vv. 47 – 53 of this chapter are full of technical Greek words which could apply to the indictment of Jesus which followed the raising of Lazarus. First we should see that the words, "*they plotted his death*" v. 53, could be more correctly rendered, "they passed a resolution" i.e. that Jesus was a wanted man and should be found.

57. *Had given orders* could better be expressed "they issued a writ". 56. *they looked for Jesus* could describe a hunt for a fugitive. 57 *should give information* (menuein) denotes the denouncing of a person named in a writ. Thus we have a package of legal terms which indicate that proceedings were taken against Jesus sometime before his arrest. In his commentary on the Greek Barrett makes no mention of the significance of these possibly because he does not regard John as a primary source. He prefers the time-table of the Synoptics.

There is a reference in Jewish sources of that period that "for forty days before the execution took place a herald went forth and cried 'he is going to be stoned because he practised sorcery and enticed Israel to apostasy. Anyone who can say anything in his favour, let him come forward and plead on his behalf'.

But since nothing was brought forward in his favour, he was hanged on the eve of the Passover".[31] This implies a considerable delay between incrimination and execution (on a cross) and this was not normal. Usually execution took place on the same day e.g. Stephen in Acts. The name of the man mentioned in the above source was Yeshu which was a common Jewish name but this independent source is interesting.

54. *Jesus left that region ... and came to a town called Ephraim.* Jesus, no doubt hearing about these latest developments, went into hiding. John alone gives details about this secret place which only an inner circle could know. Ephraim was in the hill country north of Jerusalem, about fourteen miles. There is no mention of people finding him there. He was alone with his disciples.

CHAPTER TWELVE

PREPARATION FOR DEATH

This chapter has three subjects, the Anointing, the triumphal Entry into Jerusalem and teaching about the coming death of Jesus and its results.

1 – 11. **The anointing.** All the four Gospels report this incident but with minor variations. This is to be expected from four independent writers and we have assumed throughout that John is not dependent on the other three. Matthew and Mark put this anointing after the entry into the city but Luke and John put it before. However, it should be noted that the incident is in a different context

in Luke (7:36 fol), in the early days of Our Lord's ministry. The link between Luke and other Synoptics is the host's name, Simon, presumably a former leper. Luke includes it no doubt to illustrate the theme of forgiveness but the others link it with the Passion. With his teaching about the kingship of Jesus, John might have seen Mary's gesture as an anointing before the royal entry into the city.

John seems to be the primary source because he places much of the ministry in Jerusalem where Jesus would have built up a number of acquaintances. So he could have had a circle of friends in Bethany who were associated by a common relationship with him. In the Synoptics such a circle would have had to be built up very quickly if Jesus paid his first visit to the south only just before the Passion. Luke, at least, might have extracted this incident from material before him and used it to give support to Jesus' teaching about forgiveness. The parables of the lost sheep and prodigal son are further examples of this.

Temple has no doubt that this is the reformed woman sinner of Luke and the Church has generally associated her with Mary Magdalene.

Altogether Lazarus, Mary and Martha seem to have formed an interesting household with whom Jesus had much in common. Often today an outward-looking Christian priest or lay-man may find himself involved in similar company of 'unchurchy' yet healthily interested people. They are often easier to deal with than ordinary churchgoers!

1. *Jesus came to Bethany ... there a supper.* It is not necessary to assume that the supper took place in the house of Lazarus and his sisters. Indeed we are told, "Lazarus sat among the guests". So it could well have been in the home of Simon the leper.

3. *Mary ... anointed the feet.* She sensed that a great crisis was near. It must have been clear to Jesus' friends that every time he came to the city, he was in great danger. It was more so now he had been proscribed. Luke and John say she anointed his feet but the other Gospel writers mention his head which would have been more correct for a king. In fact John says, "she smeared" the feet of Jesus and this word is used about rubbing the limbs of an athlete in a gymnasium.

6. *He was a thief.* We have no evidence of this but know he was fond of money because he handed over his master for thirty pieces of silver. Judas was the villain of the piece for the early Church and nothing too bad could be said about him.

12 – 19. **The entry into Jerusalem.** This is also reported by the Synoptics but with slight differences. There is a good case for the independence of John's account.

Robinson points out that in the Synoptists Jesus stage manages his entry on a donkey but in John the crowd takes the initiative. They come out of the city to greet him in a manner which recalls memories of the Maccabees (I Macc. 13:51). Brown says that the action of the crowd in John seems to have political overtones. Jesus is seen as a national liberator. He notes that the Greek word for "came out to greet" (eis upantesin) is used to describe the joyful reception of Greek kings into a city. There is also a parallel with the desert feeding (6:5, 15) where the crowd want to make Jesus a king.

Jesus tries to quell their ardour and sits on a donkey so that his entry is humble and not that of a king of this world. He chooses a donkey and not a war horse as Zechariah prophesied (9:9 fol). We note the disciples are not mixed up in the demonstration which may have been prompted by the report of the raising of Lazarus (v. 1.17). John in fact says that the disciples did not understand what was going on until after the resurrection (v. 16).

Robinson's remark is interesting. "For John the entry into Jerusalem with its tragic comic 'God bless the king of Israel' presents the reader in advance with the clue by which the trial of Jesus is to be interpreted, whose proceedings turn more insistently in this Gospel more than in any other upon the question, Are you the – or in what sense are you – the king of the Jews?"[32]

16. *At this time his disciples did not understand.* As they did not understand his words, Destroy this temple and in three days I will raise it up again. The Synoptists, too, note in several places the frustrating ignorance of the disciples.

19. *The Pharisees said to one another.* Despite the proscription of Jesus, his arrest seems impossible for the time being. Enthusiasm for Jesus is on a 'high' as we say, both through accounts of his raising of Lazarus and the triumphal entry.

20. *Some Greeks.* The influence of the Greeks in the Mediterranean and the Middle East was great. If the Romans had the military power, the Greeks provided the culture. There were Greek cities on the edge of Israel – the Decapolis (Ten Cities). We do not know exactly what Greeks are meant in this text. They could have been plain inquiring Greeks, Greek converts to the Jewish faith (proselytes), or Hellenistic Jews who lived in Palestine. Anyway we are to understand that a new interested element is introduced into the Gospel. John mostly deals with Jews.

Philip and Andrew, both with Greek names, are the contacts with these inquirers.

23. *The hour has come for the Son of Man to be glorified.* This can also be translated, The hour has come in order that the Son of man.... Events have built up into a great crisis as we have seen and there can only be one conclusion – arrest and death. Jesus sees this as the way to his final triumph.

In v. 32 Jesus will say that through his execution all men will be drawn to him. Here is a further statement of the theology of the Passion.

It has been the custom to link the arrival of the Greeks with this verse (24) but this is not necessary. John is not immediately concerned with the mission to the Gentiles. This verse fits in more easily with coming ordeal.

24. *A grain of wheat.* A parallel with Jesus' teaching in the Synoptics can be recognised, see especially Mark 4:26.

25. *The man who loves himself.* Here also is teaching found in the other three Gospels, see Mark 8:35.

27. *Now is my soul in turmoil.* Here we find a Gethsemane atmosphere.

This is intensified in the next verse where we are told, "a voice sounded from heaven". In Luke's account of the agony in the garden an angel is seen strengthening Jesus. Here it is the voice of God. We find similar experiences of the voice of God at the baptism of Jesus (Mark 1:11) and at the Transfiguration (Luke 9:35).

35. *Go your way while you have the light.* Lindars notes there is a parable here which forms a final appeal for them to believe before it is too late. The parable is a word picture of a traveller at sunset. He must try desperately to finish the journey before darkness overtakes him and he will lose his way.[33]

36. *Into hiding.* In these few words we understand the danger which now surrounds Jesus.

37 – 43. Here we have a summing up of the situation after three years of preaching. It is paralleled by the experience of the Old Testament prophets. We might compare the words of 2 Chronicles 36:14-16, which expressed the sad state of the Jews of the Southern Kingdom in 587 BC when the Babylonians conquered them and took them into exile. However we learn that even among the Jewish authorities Jesus had made an impression but they were afraid to stand up and be counted. To be cut off from the synagogue, as was noted earlier, meant the loss of civic and social rights.

44 – 50. *So Jesus cried aloud.* This was the final witness about his authority to the public at large. He alone can give light to a dark world because he is in complete union with God. Therefore if anybody rejects this light he is automatically judged by God.

CHAPTER THIRTEEN

THE LAST SUPPER

This might seem a wrong chapter heading because the Last Supper, as we know it, is omitted by John. However, it is clear that the action takes place within a meal – the rubric of dipping bread in wine (26) shows this. We might ask why John does not report such an important ceremony which is described by the other Gospel writers, for it became the distinctive worship of the Church from the very beginning.

The omission would be more strange if John's Gospel had been written late in the first century when the Eucharist was fully established and readers would want to know its origin. But if John is early, the need to give such details might be less important for the idea of giving thanks over a meal for many blessings (e.g. the Passover) would be taken for granted. In our day few meals start with a grace and we do not understand how natural it was to give thanks for great events and gifts when people sat down in the home for the evening meal. We know it took some years for the Eucharist to assume a definite form – after John's gospel had been completed.

Instead, the washing of feet is fully described. What are we to learn from this? It could be seen just as a lesson in humble service but it seems an elaborate device for preaching what Jesus had already taught. In his Twelve More New Testament Studies (chapter Six) Robinson suggests that it should be linked to baptism and more especially a baptism into the Lord's death aspect. So we are bidden to look at Mark 10:32 – 45. Here Jesus is teaching what his going up to Jerusalem means. The disciples think of him going up to glory – and so he is but not in the way they imagine. To share in his glory they must be prepared to drink of the cup of suffering – to be baptised into his death – for the servant is not greater than his master. The disciple must follow in the way of humiliation if he wants to share the blessedness of the coming age. What the world thinks about lordship and authority must be turned upside down. All this is summed up in the ceremony of the washing of feet where the master becomes the servant.

Jesus, then, sees his coming death as a baptism. Until this happens the Church cannot be born but once it is born then the disciples may need to drink to the full their Master's cup of suffering. This may throw some light on a difficult saying in Luke 12:49-51. Jesus is under constraint in bringing in his kingdom until he has undergone such a baptism.

When Jesus has gone his way to glory then the disciples may follow along the same path of suffering but not yet. This may explain the words of Jesus to Peter (10) and later (36). For the time being Jesus goes alone to his death and in 18:8 he can ask that the guard should let the disciples go free. Robinson's summing up of the situation is helpful. "Jesus' washing of his disciples' feet is therefore to be interpreted as a bid for their solidarity with him as he goes to his death, putting to them the challenge, Are you able to be baptised with the baptism with which I am baptised? For without that they can have no part with him, no share in his glory ... unless they are prepared to bear his cross – which is the same as to bear his love – they cannot be his disciples."

25. *Leaned back close.* "Close" is an attempt to translate the Greek word "houtōs" (see John 4:6) which can mean "just like this" and as noted above might be a stage direction given by John himself.

The supper ended and Judas having departed – it appeared to the disciples, on a natural errand – Jesus prepares his disciples for the traumatic coming events. Two words, Glory and Love, seem to require explanation for they are often insufficiently understood. Glory is not much used today except perhaps when we say a sports team is going for glory, which means they do not only want to win but to gain themselves a name or reputation. Glory in the Bible means value, weight of something (in gold perhaps) and so the importance or fame of somebody. You can see this in the description of kings in the Old Testament – Solomon, in all his glory (Matthew 6:29). The importance of a king was shown in the way he lived – palaces, fine public buildings, servants etc. We are told the Queen of Sheba was breathless at the sight of Solomon's life style, his glory. The basis of such glory could be riches. It was also the high social position of a man and the authority which went with it. Joseph says to his brothers in Genesis, "Tell my father all the glory I have in Egypt". Glory is the quality belonging to a king and is shown in his riches and power. Above all such glory belongs to God and is shown in his creation and the excellent way he has ordered everything – only man can spoil this glory. Such glory becomes known when he shows himself to man and man is overwhelmed, speechless. Moses had this vision and Isaiah and the disciples at the Transfiguration.

Man may share this glory. Jesus shared it in the highest way and was proud of it – God glorified him, brought him into his importance and power. We have the promise that if we live like Christ we shall also be glorified. What does this mean? It can be seen at a lower level when someone may be proud to serve a great man. The honour rises in proportion to that master's glory or reputation. You will hear a naval man boast that he served under a certain great captain or Admiral and if that commanding officer had a title the pride was greater. He feels that somehow the glory rubbed off on him – he was ennobled. The Old Testament looked forward to the arrival of a Messiah who would share his glory with the faithful. Our Lord now fulfills that hope and promises to share his glory with his disciples.

Love. This has become such a shallow and devalued word that it is necessary to remember that Jesus uses it in the strongest possible way. Love has been defined as doing the best for the other despite the cost – not just doing

53

something good or kind. It is best seen in a family setting where parents make sacrifices for their children and the children respond with gratitude and obedience – a desirable way of life too seldom seen in today's family.

So perfect love is that seen within the God the Father/God the Son relationship. All are called to share in that love and pass it on to each other.

CHAPTERS THIRTEEN: 31 – SIXTEEN

FAREWELL DISCOURSES

Although there is good reason for accepting an early date for John's material, as I have tried to show, and for recognising that the Gospel is written close to the events, this does not prevent us from suggesting that a later editor has been at work. This would seem to have happened with the mass of material I have called the Farewell Discourses. Several clues indicate that it is not continuous narrative. Rather does it seem that John together with his fellows are remembering all the essential information Jesus gave them for the future welfare of the Christian community. It has been suggested that there are two collections of sayings. The fact is that there is a certain amount of repetition. It does not seem to be an organised programme of instruction.

Does the shape of all this instruction owe something, I wonder, to the number of times John was called upon to tell his story? Thousands were converted in those early days of the Church and John would no doubt have been kept busy. Each time he started a new course of instruction he might have tried to improve his technique. This happens today in a school when a teacher has to repeat a lesson several times to different classes. Each time he tries to improve the presentation of his subject. Sometimes this is done after questioning by earlier classes.

Nevertheless it is a stupendous mass of teaching with several themes chasing each other and reappearing. I am reminded of a piece of music, a symphony, but not the classical style of a Haydn or Mozart where motifs or subjects are neatly developed and then discarded. Rather I have in mind the work of a Romantic composer like Tchaikowsky where major themes are sounded out, are countered by other motifs and then woven together. So the composer keeps bringing back a tune and redeveloping it with counter tunes until the end of the symphony. Think of Tchaikowsky's Sixth or Pathetique Symphony. A sombre theme is played at the beginning and this keeps reappearing but it is constantly being overtaken by more light-hearted themes. Then suddenly a breath taking purple passage takes over for a time only to be replaced by a further conflict of sad and joyful passages.

It seems to me that this might be an useful method of dealing with this flood of farewell teaching of Jesus. It would be possible to put together a verse by verse commentary but I doubt whether this would be profitable for school and parish study. We might also miss something of the grandeur of these chapters. The themes, when perceived, are simple except for a few passages which will have notes at the end. The important thing is that readers should be able to identify the main topics. So I have tried to analyse these chapters as one might take a Romantic symphony apart.

There seems to be one dominant subject which is sounded out in the last verses of Ch. 13. This is the 'going away' theme which keeps coming and going and causes perplexity and sadness among the disciples. Against this can be set a number of compensating and parallel ideas which give encouragement to those who shall follow Jesus. I hope what follows may also help today's Christian disciple to draw strength from what is the most sustained programme of teaching by Jesus.

THE MAIN SUBJECT. *The Departure of Jesus.*

13.33. Jesus says he is with them for a short while and then will go where they cannot come. The disciples might well be bewildered by this for there was something final about the Jewish idea of death. Psalm 115 summed it up; The dead praise not thee, O Lord: neither those who go down into silence. The only hope was to be allowed to rise and share the final kingdom of God on earth. The language of Jesus about going to the Father was on a different plane.

This main subject of departure is repeated throughout these chapters:

14:19. In a little while the world will see Jesus no more.

14:28. Further talk of going to the Father.

16:7. The disciples are told it is for their sake that he is leaving them.

16:16-19. The theme restated – *A little while and you shall not see me,* 16:28. The summing up. *I came from the Father and have come into the world. Now I am leaving the world again and going to the Father.*

The disciples say they understand but Jesus knows that this is not possible yet. So the farewell theme is clearly sounded. Jesus is going away and things can never be the same again.

But it is not all sadness and we find passages which tell the disciples how to measure up to the new situation.

SECONDARY THEME No. 1. *You will not be abandoned*

This is a happy subject which counters the sadness of the main subject.

14:1-3. *There are many dwelling places in my Father's house ... for I am going there to prepare a place for you.*

Lindars suggest that Jesus here is using the metaphor of a guest house. "Just as the Temple was regularly called the house of God (John 2:16) so heaven was pictured as a palace by many ancient peoples. I Enoch 39:4 fol tells of the "dwelling places of the holy and the resting-places of the righteous". It is then easy to apply to heaven a word-picture of an earthly domestic situation : someone goes on ahead to the hotel, books rooms for all the party and then returns to fetch them when all is ready".[34] We have a parallel in Mark 14:12-16 when two disciples are told to go ahead and prepare accommodation for the Passover.

14:18. *I will not leave you bereft: I am coming back to you.*

16:7. *It is for your good that I am leaving you.*

16:20 ff. *A woman in labour.* Jesus uses the analogy of a woman giving birth to a child to illustrate the joy which will finally be known.

SECONDARY THEME No. 2 *The Advocate or Holy Spirit will come*

14:15. *He (the Father) will give you another to be your Advocate.*

14:26. *He will teach you everything and will call to mind all I have told you.*

This will make them witnesses of Jesus. But under the Spirit's guidance they will also be able to make a correct assessment about the real nature of sin, about true righteousness and what is involved in judgment 16:8 ff.

So the disciples will be fully equipped for their mission in the world.

SHORT INTERJECTION – PEACE

Peace here and in the Bible is more than a mere absence of war. It indicates the well-being of daily existence, the state of the man who lives in harmony with nature, with himself, with God. It is the giving of a blessing and so has the meaning of a certain power which can remain with the disciples.

16:33. *In me you may find peace.* For John as for Paul peace is the fruit of the sacrifice of Jesus.

14:27. *Peace is my parting gift to you.* This peace is no longer linked to his presence on earth but to his victory over the world.

THE SONG OF THE VINE – 15:1–8

Suddenly after the complexity of many ideas of Ch. 14. there comes a clear lyrical passage of the parable of the Vine. It comes almost out of context and yet it teaches the importance of the disciples' lasting union with their Lord. Early Christian places of worship were to use this metaphor of the vine in their mosaics. Each disciple was to be entwined round his risen Master. So you have patterns of vine branches winding round each other. Elsewhere Jesus teaches the identity of the Father with the Son but here is expressed the relationship of a disciple to the Master. Without Jesus, nothing can be accomplished.

SECONDARY THEME No. 3. *The Suffering of the followers of Jesus.*

So far the main subject of the departure of Jesus has been met by happier thoughts of his return and the gift of the Holy Spirit. But now a more sinister note creeps in, a warning.

15:18-21. *If the world hates you, it hated me first.* This is what the disciples may expect if they carry out his work. This is spelt out more definitely in 16:1-4.

The last words of this great discourse end with a warning, 16:33. *In the world you will have trouble. But courage! The victory is mine. I have conquered the world.* Even in the middle of their hardships there will be every ground for confidence and hope.

FURTHER GENERAL MOTIF. *The Father/Son relationship.*

Throughout these chapters there runs the underlying teaching about the relationship of Jesus to his Father. This can be found elsewhere and in the other Gospels. (Luke 10:22).

Here the teaching darts in and out of the farewell narrative. Because of the close relationship of Father and Son, it can be said in 14:7-14 there is no need for special information about God because who has seen Jesus has seen the Father. Those who have stayed close to Jesus, therefore, have had a privileged position 14:22-24. The love which the Father and Son have for each other must be copied by all Jesus' disciples. It is a sacrificing love 15:11.

On the other hand to hate the Son is to hate the Father 15:24.

Finally it is the union of Father and Son which should give confidence in the coming trial.

A Note on John 16 vv 8 fol

And when he (the Holy Spirit) is come he will reprove the world of sin, and of righteousness and of judgment. Of sin because they believe not on me; of righteousness because I go to my Father and ye see me no more; of judgment because the prince of this world is judged.

I have quoted this from the old Authorised version because it was in this form that I heard it on the Fourth Sunday after Easter for many years and did not understand it. Since then there have been other attempts to bring it into modern English. The NEB has "When he comes he will confute the world and show where wrong and right and judgment lie. Both Brown and Barrett have different ideas about how to do justice to the Greek. It seems to me however that the ordinary reader might best understand this passage as a court case in the style of Perry Mason or a similar clever defending counsel. The accused has all the evidence pointing against him but his lawyer shows not only that he is innocent but turns upon another character in the court room and says, "That's the guilty man". In fact in the Gospel text the old word 'righteousness' gives the clue because the Greek word which is translated, dikaiosune, means a process of justice by which an individual is brought into court and is tried. If he is found innocent he is righteous (dikaios) or justified and he goes free. St. Paul develops this idea.

Jesus went about claiming a special authority from God and his cause, in his absence (11:47) was brought before the Jewish court. He was found guilty and disposed of as a wicked man. But the case was not over and he was declared innocent by the one who mattered, his Father. Who then was the guilty party? The Jewish religious authorities. The truth of this matter would be shown for ever after by the Holy Spirit who would act like a good defending lawyer. This was to be very important as the early Church explained what really happened at the trial and execution of their Lord.

CHAPTER SEVENTEEN

THE GREAT PRAYER OF JESUS

Temple notes that we now come to what is, perhaps, the most sacred passage even in the four Gospels – the record of the Lord's prayer of self-dedication as it lived in the memory and imagination of his most intimate friends. He divides it into three main sections.

1. The Son and the Father (1-5)

2. The Son and his disciples (6-19)

3. The Son, the disciples and the world (20-26)

There are several accounts of the prayers of Jesus in the Synoptic Gospels – Mark 1:35., 6:46, 14:32-39, 15:34. Matthew 14:23, 19:13, 26:36-44, 27:46. Luke 3:21, 5:16, 6:12, 9:18, 28 fol, 11:1, 22:41-45, 23:46.

The actual words of the prayers are not always given. In John, Jesus offers a prayer at the raising of Lazarus and now gives us in this chapter the longest prayer of all. The great prayer of Jesus comes at the same time as Gethsemane but the emphasis is different. Whereas in Gethsemane Jesus mentions the cost of obedience, in the great prayer there is no mention of sorrow or distress. Rather does it emphasise Jesus' obedience to the Father, obedience even to death.

It was the duty of the head of a Jewish family to lead in prayer especially on notable occasions. We have examples of such prayers but these are mostly of thanksgiving, often mentioning great events of the past.

The Last Supper was a watershed in the life of the disciples and the words of Jesus reflects the occasion. Here we know the relationship of the Son to the Father and the stupendous backcloth to the whole of Jesus' life.

I have not attempted a detailed commentary on this chapter but have commented on its three sections.

1-5. Jesus talks about his own commission and the fulfilment of it. He addresses the Father, recalls his obedient completion of the work entrusted to him in the world. He prays that his approaching suffering may be the decisive means by which he glorifies the Father and the Father glorifies the Son.

6-19. Jesus now turns his attention to his disciples upon whom the weight of witness in the world is about to fall. They have been called out of the world and will bear its attacks. So far Jesus has watched over them and shown them the truth. Now he is going away, they will be under great pressure and he prays they will all be one in their mission to the world. We have the use of the word 'consecrate' (agiazon in Greek) which means to make holy. A holy person is set apart for a sacred duty and this is exactly what happened to Jesus when he came into the world. He was On His Majesty's Service and the disciples must be the same.

19. *For their sakes I consecrate myself.* This means that Jesus will now re-enter the divine life so that he may take his disciples with him and so bring them into the glory of God.

20-26. Jesus finally prays about those who in future will believe because of the disciples' teaching. He prays that they will be united in love both with each other and also with the Father and Son. This will make the world believe in the mission of the Son. Everyone, therefore, will be caught up in the divine loving family life and will share God's glory.

Jesus ends by reviewing the result of his ministry. The world did not recognise the hand of God. But some believers understood what was happening and have found and will find eternally truth and love.

CHAPTER EIGHTEEN

THE FINAL CONFLICT

You could say that John now continues the narrative of the trial, arrest and execution of the Lord for there is a good case for saying that in Chapter Eleven the decisive trial of Jesus had taken place in his absence. As far as the Jewish authorities were concerned, Jesus was a guilty person who had to be caught and punished. It was this catching which was the difficult part for it was clear from the former visits Jesus had made to Jerusalem that he had many supporters there. The arrest of such a person might well cause an uprising and this the Jews were unwilling to risk.

Thus the role of Judas was all-important for he knew the quiet places Jesus used for prayer during his visits to the city. There is here, by the way, confirmation of the fact that Jesus was as much at home in the city as in Galilee. He knew where to go when he wanted to be alone – note v.2. He often met there with his disciples. This seems to vindicate John's chronology against that of the Synoptics who show Jesus coming to Jerusalem only at the end of his ministry. Generally one feels John is more conversant with conditions and the political situation than the others. He writes from being very close to the events.

1. *There was a garden there.* Matthew and Mark name the place as Gethsemane. Luke calls it a place on the Mount of Olives but John pinpoints it more accurately. It was just across the Kedron valley. Many a modern pilgrim to the Holy Land will have done the Maundy Thursday walk. After dark the procession leaves the church of the Last Supper, passes out of the walls of the city and then carefully picks its way down the hill to the bottom where there is the remains of a dried-up stream. A motorway now passes beside it and pilgrims have to cross this to the other side where Gethsemane is marked. It was here Jesus retired to pray and it was here that Judas found him with his disciples. It is a short distance from the city.

3. *A detachment of soldiers.* John here significantly differs from the other Gospels in naming the actual men who arrested Jesus. The Synoptists call them just a 'crowd' and Luke improbably suggests the chief priests etc came out in person. But John calls them temple police or constables of the court (see Matthew 5:25). John uses the Greek word huperete in a judicial sense whereas the other gospels use doulos, servant. But as well as these temple police, John refers to a detachment of Roman soldiers under a tribune v.12 *chiliarchos.* The word for detachment, *speira,* would indicate 600 men but it would be wrong to suppose they were all withdrawn from duty in the city to arrest one man. So we may suppose it was just a detachment of the cohort.

Some commentators have argued that John wrongly names the Romans as part of the arresting party but we may remember that they were expecting to arrest a terrorist or freedom fighter. As Robinson says, "Who would have arrested Barabbas but the Romans?"[35] They would also have taken the precaution of doing it in some strength. The shameful thing was that the Jews took the initiative. In fact the Jews were not above using the Roman power to achieve their own ends. They could then bring Jesus before Pilate as one disturbing the peace. Robinson also points out that the weapons carried on this occasion are evidence for the kind of troops used, cudgels (zuloi) of the temple constables and the swords of the soldiers.

6. *They drew back and fell to the ground.* Commentators tend to explain this as a normal reaction to a divine appearance or theophany but I suggest that it a complete surprise of the troops on finding they are not being met with fierce resistance. The guard move forward and then find there is nothing to attack, except a few unarmed men. In the dark they stop and those coming up behind them push them over. Anybody who has been on night exercises with infantry will know how easy it is to fall over troops which have suddenly pulled up.

8. *Let these others go.* John shows that the disciples did not just run away but were dismissed by the Lord. Only Peter puts up resistance. Note that John alone can identify individuals of the guard, indicating perhaps years of trading with priestly personnel.

12. *They took him to Annas.* The Romans at this stage were being law enforcement officers for the Jews. So far, Jesus had done nothing to warrant further Roman interest – there had been no fighting. Some scholars have thought that John is wrong here and that the Romans, having helped with the arrest, would not want Jesus out of their hands but if we look at Acts 21-23 we see a parallel incident. A centurion sent to quell a riot thought Paul was a terrorist but when he found it was matter of Jewish Law he handed him over this time to the Sanhedrin. Here Jesus was handed over to the high priest, not for trial which would have been illegal in the night, but so that a decision could be made about the kind of charges which could be framed against him.

15. *Jesus was followed by Simon Peter.* At this point we have the account of Peter's denial. There are differences about this in the four gospels but this was to be expected in such a confused situation. However, John gives such convincing information that you must conclude either that he has exceptional literary flair or was very close to the action. Generally the narrative shows an intimate knowledge of the high priest's palace and, as has been suggested, this could be due to John's business connection.

16. *The disciple who was acquainted with the High Priest* or a friend of the High Priest. Apart from the business connection, he had a possible link with the Temple because of family connections. (See Introduction – A Fishy Business).

19. *The High Priest questioned Jesus.* There has been much debate about what exactly took place at the trial of Jesus. It is clear we must dismiss the idea that the Jewish authorities hurriedly convened an illegal court and hastened through a conviction of Jesus. This would have been against their Law which they would not dare break even in this emergency. As has been indicated before much is explained if the real trial had taken place before (11:43-57). The actual verdict could be given later when the accused had been confronted with his crime. It would seem this took place when Jesus was examined by the High Priest.

There have been attempts to work out the case of the Jews versus Jesus but it must be obvious that through the very nature of his divine mission Jesus would be on a collision course with Jewish authority at several points. His relationship with God his father was not likely to be understood and his criticism of their interpretation of the Law touched a most sensitive spot.

As I noted earlier (p. 48) there is a Jewish document dating from the early centuries AD which mentions a man Yeshu who was executed after a delay of forty days. It said that this man practised sorcery and this would fit in with the charge that Jesus cured people with the help of the forces of evil (Beelzebub). Luke notes the charge that he subverted the nation. Matthew 27:63 used the word 'deceiver'. Sorcery was one of the capital crimes among the Jews – the Law was very strong against it but it was not a charge the Romans were likely to take seriously. But the charge of the leading the people astray was more promising and this was mentioned also in the same Jewish document quoted above – 'because he practised sorcery and *enticed Israel to apostasy*'. This could involve political unrest and that concerned the Romans very much everywhere. So it was the Romans who had to be persuaded to execute Jesus. Therefore John passes quickly over the appearance of Jesus before the High Priest, possibly because it was not important for the final act. Since he was elsewhere in the courtyard at the time, he had no information and, as we have observed, John prefers personal experience.

28. From Caiaphas Jesus was led into the Governor's headquarters'. The Jews having been prosecutors now become defendants because they have to satisfy Pilate that he should execute Jesus. Here John has much to say. If he was able to get entry into the High Priest's house the night before, perhaps his business contacts took him into Pilate's palace as well. Romans also would need to buy fish! We certainly seem to have an authentic report on the proceedings.

33. Are you the king of the Jews? This was the chief point a governor, trying to preserve order in an occupied land, would want to know. Rival kings had a habit of rousing support and from this riots follow. But Pilate is not convinced that he has a dangerous political rival in front of him and refused to take action.

CHAPTER NINETEEN

THE CONFLICT ENDED

1. Pilate ... had him flogged. John differs from Mark and Matthew who both report a flogging immediately before the crucifixion. But flogging was often done before further examination. Paul was flogged as a preliminary to investigation (Acts 22:24 ff). We know that today some governments torture prisoners to get more information out of them.

6. I find no case against him. The flogging produced no more evidence and Pilate wants to set Jesus free. This redoubles the efforts of the Jews to have him put to death and they use a final weapon of reminding the governor that he could well lose his job if he allowed this small matter to spark off trouble in his province. Power was held very precariously in the Roman Empire and there were many men aspiring to promotion. There were many perks to be had as a governor of any area and these were not to be lightly sacrificed. The Romans anyway were a pragmatic, unsentimental race and Pilate would not have agonised unduly over one insignificant Jew. So he gives the Jews what they want and sends Jesus to his death.

If we doubt Pilate's vulnerability we need only study the struggle for power in the Roman Empire. Readers of Robert Graves' mostly accurate novels about the early Emperors (Claudius the God etc) will understand the intrigue which went on in the court of Tiberius. Sejanus who had risen from the ranks of the Army dominated the court after Tiberius had withdrawn from Rome to his villa in Capri. He promoted favourites to commands, including Pilate. In 31 AD he went too far and was executed but the preceding years had been full of uncertainty. The Jewish authorities would have known the vicissitudes in Rome and did not hesitate to exploit it.

The Synoptic Gospels say that Pilate executed Jesus to please the people but this does not fit in with the character Josephus, a later historian, gave him. It is more likely that he had his eye on the Roman scene and did not want to hazard his reputation unnecessarily. Here we have a further example of John's excellent knowledge of the political scene.

13 ff. *He brought Jesus out and took his seat on the tribunal.* Here again John fixes the place, time and date – the Pavement, the eve of the Passover, about noon. It is no longer possible to locate the exact place of the governor's palace because it was destroyed by Titus in 70 AD. The word for tribunal in Greek means raised platform. Pilgrims today are shown the Pavement at the Ecce Homo convent. This is probably not the genuine place but it gives an idea of what the stone paving looked like.

15. *We have no king but Caesar.* Robinson notes that this shows an obsequiousness which would not have been credible after the Jewish revolt of 66-70 AD and adds that if it does come from a later period, it is a masterly piece of historical reconstruction.[36]

It would seem that John gives the best programme of the Passion and we might here give a summary:

1. Several weeks before the Passover Jesus is tried in his absence by a court of religious authorities and found guilty.
2. A warrant is issued for his arrest.

3. Jesus is elusive while he completes his work.

3. An unexpected lucky break comes for the authorities when Judas promises to betray his master.

4. He guides the troops and police to Gethsemane and Jesus is arrested under cover of dark

5. He is taken to the High Priest so that his guilt may be confirmed.

6. The decision is made that he should die but this will be in the hands of the Romans and must wait until the morning.

7. When Pilate is ready the Jews appear before him to present their case. They have to defend their request for execution. Pilate is unwilling to satisfy them.

8. Pilate's first examination of Jesus reveals no reason for condemnation.

9. Pilate seeks a way out by offering the release of a prisoner but the Jews ask for Barabbas.

10. Pilate orders a flogging to extract any undiscovered information.

11. This reveals nothing and Pilate again resists presure but finally gives way to political blackmail.

12. Jesus is condemned and led away to crucifixion.

The time of day for this is uncertain. Mark's statement that it was nine in the morning is too early for the catalogue of events to have taken place. Noon or after is more likely.

It is just likely that Mark, despite his early timing, could give a clue to the time. In 15:21 he says that Simon of Cyrene was pressed into carrying the cross "as he was on his way in from the country". Since work in the fields outside the city stopped at noon on the eve of the Passover, this could confirm a timing of midday. It would mean, however, a discarding of the idea that Simon was an expatriate visitor from North Africa.

There has been disagreement among scholars about the actual day but if we follow the chronology given at the beginning of this book we shall find that the year 30 AD was possibly the year of the Passion. In this year the afternoon when the passover lambs were killed (Nisan 14) fell on a Friday and this is what John says 19:14. Robinson has gone further and worked out that in 30 AD Nisan 14 fell on April 7th.

THE CRUCIFIXION

17. *Carrying his own cross.* John does not mention the help given by Simon but this does not mean the incident did not take place. Simon and his family may not have been known in John's community.

The place of a skull. There have been several attempts to locate the original Golgotha but the traditional site is probably the correct one. This is now marked by the huge Church of the Holy Sepulchre which covers both the place of crucifixion and resurrection.

It would have been just outside the city walls of that time and close enough for people to read the inscription. John also says the tomb was close at hand and it is possible still to see the remains of ancient tombs on the circumference of the present church.

19. *Pilate wrote an inscription.* So far from being anxious to please the Jews, Pilate turns the execution to his own advantage by the insult implicit in the words and the Jews try to get it changed.

23 ff. John describes the final scene from close at hand whereas the Synoptists say that followers looked on from afar. John is on the spot and notes the details of the last minutes, such as the dividing of the cloak and the little group which stood at the foot of the cross. So John narrates the division of the prisoner's clothes in greater detail than other accounts. He shows the execution was done by four soldiers (quaternion), the usual number for such a duty. Also as Dodd points out, Psalm 22 does not control the narrative in John as it does in the others. He just mentions the connection as an after-thought.

25. *But meanwhile near the cross ... stood his mother.* John is also near enough to hear Jesus commending his mother to his care. His own home would imply somewhere in the city.

28. *I thirst.* John also notes the detail of the giving of wine to the dying man. Hyssop was a small bushy plant and would not have served a useful purpose here. The reading, hysso, the Greek for javelin is probably to be preferred.

31. *They requested Pilate to have the legs broken.* The breaking of the victim's legs is confirmed by the skeleton of a man crucified in the first century AD which was dug up in Jerusalem. Both the legs had been smashed. This same skeleton shows that the nails were driven through the wrists and ankles. If they had gone through the palms the body could not have been supported. Robinson points out this is attested by the Shroud of Turin, if it is genuine. It also confirms the piercing of the side. In any case this latter is attested strongly by John and we must accept that he was there.

A flow of blood and water. John here gives the hard medical facts of such a death. A person in such a hanging position would have found it difficult to breathe. Water would have formed and this would be released by such a blow in the side. John is anxious that we should know that Jesus died as any other man might, under those conditions. It is indeed graphic evidence.

THE BURIAL

38. *After that.* John at this stage is less precise than Mark and Matthew who indicate it is the evening but he does say, "because it was the eve of the sabbath".

Joseph of Arimathaea. All the Gospel writers give information about him. Matthew 27:57 says he was a man of means and had become a disciple. Mark 15:43 says he was a respected member of the Council and was eagerly awaiting the kingdom of God. Luke 23:50 ff states not only that he was a member of the Council but was a good upright man who had not agreed with its policy and the action taken. John now says he was a secret disciple of Jesus because he feared the Jews. It is possible to see in John's undeveloped account a sign of the primitive date. He then goes on to say simply that Joseph came and took the body away.

39. *He was joined by Nicodemus.* This is John's special contribution to the description of the burial.

A mixture of myrrh and aloes, more than half a hundredweight. This would have been about seventy pounds in our weight and has been thought excessive but we need to understand that the spices were not meant to anoint the body but to preserve it and keep it sweet-smelling over the sabbath. If the spices were packed round the body much would have been needed. The weight stated by John is reasonable if it was a final tribute from a rich man.

Nicodemus. Only in John does this figure appear. We might trace the development of his relationship with Jesus. He comes to be taught by the Lord, was impressed enough to defend him in the Sanhedrin 7:50-52 and now joins another secret disciple in the burial.

41. *There was a garden.* If John is not precise about the timing, he gives us detail about the place of burial. It was in a garden near the place of crucifixion, how near can be seen in the present church which covers both sites.

This simple, straightforward narrative of John gives confidence that he was very much in touch with the burial arrangements. If he had taken the mother of Jesus away, he would need to keep her informed that everything had been done decently. It means a lot to mothers to know their children have a proper resting place.

CHAPTER TWENTY

THE RESURRECTION

We now come to the climax of the Gospel for, without the resurrection of Jesus, there would be no Christian Church at all. We are then fortunate in having John as our guide through this great event because he has already shown himself a close observer of the ministry of Our Lord. His narrative is the more exciting if we accept he is giving his witness at an early rather than late date. He no longer becomes dependent on other sources but relates his own experience.

Barrett notes there are two Easter traditions 1) the empty tomb 2) the appearances of the risen Lord to his followers and congratulates John on combining the two expertly but if we assume an early date for the Johannine material, we do not need any artificial construction.

1. *Early ... while it was still dark*. But it was not so dark that she could not see what had happened. It would seem Mary Magdalene was not alone for in v.2 she says '*we do not know ...*'. If she had to go back into the city to find Peter and John, it would not have taken long because the burial place was just outside the walls.

We should note that there was no expectation that Jesus had risen. The only answer could be that somebody had removed the body. No doubt they thought it was the Jewish authorities just as the Jews spread the story that the disciples had taken it.

5. *He peered in*. The Greek word also means 'stooped down' and this he would have done for the old tombs which can still be seen round Jerusalem are like small caves in the side of rock formation. There is the inner chamber with just about enough room for the body and an outer entrance lobby where a relative could crouch and pay respects. There would not have been much room for two men on that first Easter morning!

7. *He saw the linen wrappings lying*. Now follows John's careful description of the first Easter scene. One commentator (Bernard) wrote. "That the first disciple to note the presence of the grave clothes in the tomb did not actually go into it first, is not a matter which would seem worth noting to any one except the man who refrained from entering".[37] Dodd says of this passage that there is nothing quite like it in the gospels and asks if there was anything quite like it in all ancient literature.[38]

There seem to be two cloths with different Greek names. There was the *othonia* or large sheet and this acted like a modern coffin. It would be wrapped round, but not mummy-like. When the body had been anointed properly, this sheet would be tied at top and bottom with strips of cloth. In due course the body would decay but the bones would be contained within the sheet and eventually put into an ossuary. Such a small box of bones from the first century AD have been found on the Mount of Olives. They belonged to a man named Johanan.

The other cloth is called the *soudarion* by John. This was a sweat cloth or handkerchief, used also for Lazarus (John 11:44). There we read his face was bound round with it. In the case of Jesus the Greek tells us it was over his head. Robinson says the only thing which could be described as going round the face and over the head is a jaw band and this we know was certainly used in Jewish burial customs.[39] The purpose was to stop the chin from sinking lower, as the Mishnah says. Such a band could be made by folding a handkerchief in a triangle, like a bandage. Robinson goes on to say that the cloth was still in this shape when found on Easter morning, 'rolled up in an oval loop', as the Greek entetuligmenon could be translated (7), having just slipped off the jaw. As John accurately reports, it lay separately from the main shroud.

11 fol. Now follows the appearances of Jesus to his followers. The first is to Mary Magdalene who had remained behind in the garden after Peter and John had returned to the city, no doubt to discuss this new development with other disciples.

The meeting of Mary with the risen Lord must be one of the most heart-warming in the gospels and the two words, 'Mary' and 'Rabbuni' ring out as the true words of greeting.

17. *Do not touch me.* There has been much discussion about this sentence. Barrett's comment that Jesus is discouraging her from trying to recapture the past by trying to keep hold of him is credible. The resurrection has made possible a more spiritual relationship between Jesus and his disciples.

19. *Late that evening.* Only Luke with his account of the walk to Emmaus supplies a true parallel to this further appearance on the first Easter day. Matthew has complicated the issue by reporting that Jesus told his disciples to go away into Galilee whereas Luke and John place the appearances in Jerusalem. A Jewish rabbi, Pinchas Lapide, in a recent book on the Resurrection of Jesus, notes that the word Galil in Hebrew means nothing but environs or region and thinks this designates the area of Bethany to the east of Jerusalem where Mary and Martha lived.[40] This gains plausibility by a reference of Tertullian (2nd cent. AD) to "Galilee, an area in Judaea." Galil is still used in modern Israel for the designation of any area.

Peace. As noted earlier 'Peace' means more than quiet. The normal meaning, "May all be well with you" now in Christian minds takes on a deeper meaning. All indeed was well because death had been conquered.

22. *Then he breathed on them.* It has been suggested that John intends to indicate an event of tremendous importance, parallel to that of the creation of man in Genesis. This might be possible if John was written late but it seems an unnecessary elaboration if this is straight early narrative.

23. *If you forgive.* This is an extension of the ministry of Jesus which had brought reconciliation or forgiveness. We may remember Our Lord's words, "Thy sins be forgiven thee" (Mark 2:5) and see this power now given to the disciples. The granting of pardon to the penitent has always been an important part of the priestly ministry in the Catholic Church.

However we should not see this commission in isolation. Just as Jesus is the representative of his Father to bring reconcilation and peace to the world so the apostles are sent out in the same way. Jesus is the great Apostle, the one *sent* by the Father and his disciples are given a share in the apostleship. In his great prayer in the Upper Room (John 17:18) Jesus had prayed, As thou didst send me into the world, so I have sent them into the world". Now comes the moment of their actual sending. As they preach they will be the means of grace to some whose sins can be forgiven but of blindness to others who reject them. Their sins would be retained. This was the same division which Jesus observed in his preaching.

24. *One of the twelve, Thomas.* The story of doubting Thomas is well known. Perhaps it was included for the sake of the final sentence, "happy are they who never saw me and yet have found faith" for it would have referred to many of John's hearers.

An attempt to discredit the truth of the Thomas story by suggesting that since Jesus was tied to the cross and not nailed there were no wounds to be seen has been balanced by the finding of the bones of a man crucified in the first century AD. Nails had been driven through his wrists and ankles. (See earlier note 19:3).

30. *There were indeed many other signs..* The Gospel, as such, seems to end here. John states his authority for writing – as Luke did at the beginning of his Gospel – and ends by showing that receiving the Gospel means commitment. Life can never be the same again. "These things" are written that you may believe and have faith in Jesus, in his name. Scholars have seen Chapter 21 as an epilogue which contains important lessons for the growth and life of the Church.

CHAPTER TWENTY ONE

EPILOGUE

Despite the building of vast high-rise hotels at Tiberias at the southern end of the Sea of Galilee, the lake has changed little from the time of Jesus. For many a modern pilgrim it is the highlight of his visit to the Holy Land and he is entranced by the view especially at dawn and sunset. In the early morning small ships still set out to fish in the well-supplied waters and catches are landed along the coast where the lake gently washes the rocky beach.

Here is the scene of the last meeting the risen Lord had with his disciples and small churches mark the places where the load of fish was landed and Jesus gave the command to Peter, Feed my sheep. When today the Eucharist is celebrated in these churches or in the open it is as if the centuries have been rolled back and we are taking part in the events of this last chapter of John's Gospel.

It is, therefore, a shock to realise from the evidence of the text alone that this chapter has been added on to the rest just as the first verses of Chapter One seem to form an introduction. Barrett calls this chapter 21 the Appendix. Certainly the Gospel seems originally to have ended with vv. 30 and 31 of the previous chapter. Here we are told that the book has been written so that we might hold the faith that Jesus is the Christ, the Son of God, and that through this faith we may possess life by his name. One could not want a better rounding off of a piece of writing.

Yet we should not lightly dismiss the material in this chapter. Lightfoot notes that the textual evidence for it is all but unanimous and that it agrees in style with the rest of the Gospel. Robinson says that this is as vivid in its details of name, place and number as anything in this or any other Gospel. He quotes Gardner-Smith as saying that 'it was more primitive than the traditions embodied in the First and Third Gospels'.[41] It would seem to represent a very early form of the tradition of the resurrection. The last verse of the apocryphal Gospel of Peter hints at this appearance: "But I Simon Peter, and Andrew, my brother, took our nets and went to the sea; and with us was Levi, son of Alphaeus, whom the Lord ..." here the text breaks offs.

I find the suggestion of an American scholar, Brevard Charles interesting.[42] In his book, The New Testament As Canon, he has much to say about the way the books of the New Testament were edited and put into the best possible shape. He says that the writers were very conscious of the stupendous revelation they had been given in the person of Jesus and wanted to pass it on in the very best way. Of Chapter 21 he says, "the chapter offers an excellent example of canonical shaping which reflects on issues addressing the mission of the church in future generations, indeed from the resurrection to the return of Christ". He continues, "I would argue ... that the chapter has been shaped with the entire

Gospel already in mind and with a conscious theological purpose". He seems to be saying that the Gospel was finally edited so that everything else rested upon Chapter 21 as its foundation. Charles writes, "The Fourth Gospel ends, not with another attempt to create faith in the resurrected Christ but rather with the issue of how Christ's disciples were to minister to the world in the light of the resurrection" He further suggests that this chapter functions as an application of the Farewell Discourse in Chapter 14 – 17. He seems to be saying that in this chapter we find stage directions for presenting the rest of the material to the world.

With all this in mind we may look at this chapter.

We find that some of the disciples had gone fishing and note that Thomas and Nathaniel have now joined the usual band of fishermen. They catch nothing and then see a figure beside the lake who asks if they have caught anything. The question in Greek expects the answer No and this is what they say. They are told to cast the net on the right side of the boat. We might say here that the right side was thought to be the lucky side. So it proves for they soon have their net full. They then recognise the figure as Jesus and Peter, first clothes himself decently and then swims to land. They all follow in the boat and find food cooking on the fire. They are told to add some of the fish they have caught to this and so drag the net to share and count the fish.

One hundred and fifty and three was the size of the catch. Attempts have been made to draw lessons from this number but with little result. It is possible they counted automatically to ensure everybody had his fair share.

After the meal, Jesus shows his confidence in Peter by telling him to feed the sheep and the disciple whom Jesus loved is established in the role of being an authentic witness to Christ.

So we may learn from all this:

The Church must be like fishermen and be catching men. It must go for growth. The work of Christ described by John must always be taken to the outside world. It is a never ending missionary enterprise.

The Eucharist must be the central gathering for the new family of Christ. The invitation of Jesus, Come and dine, must be passed on to all believers. We know this quickly happened for in Acts 2 we read that the baptised met daily for the breaking of bread.

A continuing ministry was inaugurated by Jesus to provide pastoral care for believers. The witness of the written Gospel was to be accepted, *"we know his testimony is true"*. But more than this the major emphasis is to stress the continued presence of Jesus with his disciples. Brevard Charles writes: "The stories of the fishing and the meal function as transparencies to assure succeeding generations of Christ's ability to meet their needs".

So the foundation of the Church may be seen as Christ who meets us at a special meal. It is the work of disciples to go out and bring more people into the Christian family. They do this by faithfully passing on the Gospel which is a reliable record of Christ's saving work.

I conclude by saying that where this foundation has been faithfully followed, the Church has flourished. Only when we have failed to accept the Gospels as reliable material has the Church faltered in its mission.

AN OLD TESTAMENT BACKGROUND TO THE GOSPELS

By the end of the first book of the Bible, Genesis, we have met one of the main characters of the book, **Abraham**. His part in the Jewish scheme of things was to leave the sophisticated city life of Ur in modern Iraq with his family and go into the desert. Here he met the one God who made a covenant with him. If Abraham was faithful to this one God, he would be made the father of a special people who one day would possess the land we now call Israel. Moreover through him all nations of the earth would be blessed. This faith in one God only was to be the distinctive belief of the Hebrew people. Meanwhile there were dangers ahead and when we meet the second Jewish hereo, **Moses**, the Hebrews were trapped in Egypt as slaves.

About 1200 BC this Moses led a band of Jews out of Egypt where they had been slaves. In the wilderness they seem to have rejoined tribes of similar blood relationship. Moses formed them into a nation, based upon a Covenant (agreement or marriage) with a God who was One, Holy and without human or animal image. At this point it is worth considering that while much of the Christian world in the last century or more has been agonising about the Genesis story of the physical creation of the world, the more important story for the Jews of the Old Testament was the creation of the People of God. If this people kept the Law of the ten Commandments, God would make them his special people and use them to bring other people to serve him. For the time being they remained nomads but they invaded Palestine, gradually conquering the inhabitants and settled down to city life. In this conquest **David** was a leading figure. He united all the Jewish tribes, defeated the powerful Philistines and chose Jerusalem as the capital city. His son, Solomon, built the Temple and other fine buildings and cities.

After his reign, the country split into two kingdoms, North and South, and drifted away from the true religion by worshipping other local gods.

Prophets, preaching statesmen, tried to call them back to the one true God but suffered badly in giving this unpopular message. *Note this theme in the Old Testament where the good man suffers because he speaks against the evil of his age.*

Between 700 and 600 BC great outside nations invaded the Jews and deported many. Some were taken to Babylon where they managed to survive as a people because they kept their Jewish customs and met in synagogues to hear the Law and also encouraging messages from preachers or prophets. During this Exile they began to put together the first five books of the Bible. About 500 BC they were allowed to return to Palestine where they rebuilt their city of Jerusalem and the Temple despite opposition from people of the land, Jews who had not been deported with the rest but who had intermarried with the invader and taken over the country. These later were called Samaritans, half caste Jews. All the Jews were now ruled by the Persians who had conquered the Babylonians. They became a very narrow, exclusive people and forgot their mission to other nations.

However, the Persians in turn were defeated by the Greeks and in c.180 BC the Greek army entered Palestine and tried to destroy Jewish religion. They forbade the keeping of the Law and placed the figure of a Greek god in the Temple (Abomination of Desolation – *Mark 13:14*). Some Jews – the priestly or Sadducee party – accepted and even welcomed the Greek way of life but a band of freedom fighters, the Maccabees, fought desperately for the Law and the Jewish faith and after many battles drove the Greeks out of Palestine. These patriots are considered to be the first members of the Pharisee party. There now followed a time of peace when it was possible for the Jews to govern themselves but their rulers so quarrelled among themselves that some pious men were disgusted and despaired of setting up God's kingdom on earth by themselves. They went off to live a monastic life in the desert to wait for God to send down a new age or kingdom upon the earth. We know much about these people because in 1948 many of their writings were discovered near the Dead Sea. They were called Essenes. We can read that they built up a vivid, fantastic picture of the coming of the Kingdom of God. They believed He would send armies of angels from heaven to destroy foreigners and ungodly people. A great leader would bring in a new age of peace and prosperity for the chosen ones. These colourful and military ideas about the kingdom of God were widely held in the time of Jesus and it was necessary for him to show that his kingdom different entirely. It was a kingdom of peace which fought only against evil, sickness and ignorance.

Meanwhile as we have seen above, two main religious parties had developed, the Sadducees (Priests) and Pharisees (Teachers of the Law). This Law had become a very complicated set of regulations and no longer dealt with simple matters of everyday life. The study of it had become an intellectual exercise beyond the capabilities of the ordinary Jew who was reckoned to have little chance of entering the coming kingdom of God.

The Romans took over Palestine in 60 BC and made it part of the province of Syria within their great empire. It was administered by a Roman governor and a garrison of soldiers. The Jews hated this occupation and the Zealot party constantly rebelled against it. The Romans allowed the Jews to have their own kings drawn from the Herod family but these had little actual power. The Romans divided the country into four parts and put a king over each area. Since the Herods did not like each other there was little chance of their uniting to throw out the Romans. Jesus was born in the reign of Herod the Great and Herod Antipas had John the Baptist executed. Herodians were the members of the households of different kings and had little or no authority. Moreover they were disliked by the ordinary Jew because the Herods were not a truly Jewish family.

So Jesus of Nazareth had to carry out his ministry in a very difficult political situation. Any teacher who gained popularity would be expected to lead a campaign against the foreign occupiers of their Holy Land and this Jesus refused to do.

BOOKS CONSULTED

Barrett C.K.	The Gospel According to John	SPCK
Brown R.E.	Gospel According to John	Anchor Bible
Childs Brevard	The New Testament as Canon	SCM
Dodd C.H.	Interpretation of the Fourth Gospel	Cambridge
Harvey A.E.	Jesus and the Constraints of History	Duckworth
Hoskyns/Davey	The Fourth Gospel	Faber and Faber
Lapide Pinchas	The Resurrection of Jesus	SPCK
Lindars Barnabas	The Gospel of John	New Century Bible
Lightfoot R.H.	St. John's Gospel	Oxford
Robinson J.A.R.	Priority of John	SCM
	Twelve N.T. Studies	
	More N.T. Studies	
	Redating the N.T.	
Schillbeeckx	Christ	Collins
Temple William	Readings in St. John's Gospel	Macmillan
Vermes	Dead Sea Scrolls in English	Pelican
Rowland C.	Christian Origins	SPCK
McKenzie	Dictionary of the Bible	Chapman
Jerome	Biblical Commentary	Chapman
Darton M.	Modern Concordance to the New Testament	Darton,
	Longman, Todd	
Hengel M.	The Johannine Question	SCM 1989

INDEX

1. Page 118.
2. Page 326.
3. Ed. Harvey A.E. (SPCK). Chap. 1.
4. SCM. 1989.
5. Duckworth 1982. Page 1.
6. Cambridge University Press 1977. Page 4.
7. Robinson J.A.T. Priority of John SCM 1985. Page 30.
8. Brown R.E. The Gospel According to John. Anchor Bible 1966. xlvii.
9. Hengel. Op.cit. Page 124.
10. SCM. 1984. Page 121.
11. Op.cit. Pages 160 ff.
12. Robinson J.A.T. Redating the New Testament. SCM 1976. Page 264.
13. Strabo. Geography 16. 764.
14. Ed. Wilkinson. Egeria's Travels. SPCK 1971. Page 38.
15. Robinson J.A.T. Twelve New Testament Studies. SCM 1962. Chap. 8.
16. Op.cit. Page 141.
17. Josephus. Jewish War. Book IV. 473.
18. Geoffrey Bles. 1947. Page 163.
19. St. John's Gospel. Oxford 1956. Page 114.
20. Op.cit. Vol. 1. Page 175.
21. Fernseed and Elephants. Fount 1975. Page 108.
22. Barrett C.K. The Gospel According to John. SPCK 1955. Page 293.
23. Page 158 ff.
24. Op.cit. Page 195.
25. Op.cit. Page 202.
26. Priority of John. Page 89.
27. MacMillan 1945. Page 166.
28. Hoskyns and Davey. The Fourth Gospel. Faber 1940. Page 395.
29. Op.cit. 221.
30. Op.cit. Page 395.
31. Robinson J.A.T. Priority of John. Pages 225 ff.
32. Op.cit. Pages 229 ff.
33. Gospel of John. New Century Bible Commentary 1972. Page 435.
34. Op.cit. Page 470.
35. Op.cit. 241.
36. Op.cit. 266.
37. Bernard. John Vol. II. ICC 1928. Page 660.
38. Dodd C.H. Historical Tradition in the Fourth Gospel. Cambridge 1966. Page 148.
39. Op.cit. Pages 291 ff.
40. SPCK 1981. Page 113.
41. Op.cit. Page 295.
42. Op.cit. Page 141.